The Last White Empresses

The
Last White Empresses

by
Clive Harvey

Published by

Carmania Press
Unit 212, Station House, 49, Greenwich High Road, London, SE10 8JL.

© Carmania Press and Clive Harvey.
ISBN 0-9543666-3-8. First published 2004.
British Library Cataloguing for Publication Data.
A Catalogue Record for this book is available from The British Library.
Artwork production by Alan Kittridge.
Printed by The Amadeus Press, Cleckheaton.

Contents

FRONT COVER
Stephen Card's nostalgic painting of *Empress of Britain* and *Empress of Canada* (in the middle distance) at Funchal on the 17th February, 1962 recalls the post-War prime of the Canadian Pacific passenger fleet. *Captain Stephen J. Card.*

INSIDE FRONT COVER
Promoting the St. Lawrence route: an advertisement for Canadian Pacific, 'the World's Most Complete Transportation System'. *Author's collection.*

BACK COVER
Fashions in ship design may change, but a perfectly proportioned liner will always please the eye. *Apollon* at Spitsbergen in 1999. *Author's collection.*

Introduction

Although I wasn't quite eight years old at the time, I still remember very clearly the morning of the 18th April, 1957. When I went down for breakfast, my mother told me how she and my father had considered waking me the previous night so that I could see a television documentary about the new Canadian Pacific liner. "Oh, but why didn't you?" I cried. "No," she said, "we thought it was better to let you sleep." Why I should have remembered such a minor incident remains a mystery. However, it was not until researching for this book that I discovered its significance. The BBC had made a documentary programme on the launching and subsequent fitting out of *Empress of England* and this had been screened on the eve of her maiden voyage departure for Canada: it was appropriately entitled *Tomorrow she sails*. All these years later, I am still hoping that I may have an opportunity to see it!

About seven years or so later, I became aware that a couple in the nearby village were emigrating to Canada. This was not a piece of news that interested me much until I discovered that they were sailing on *Empress of Canada*. Then I was consumed with envy.

By the time that I took to cruising, the Canadian Pacific passenger liner fleet was no more and the last three 'White Empresses' had been dispersed: *Empress of Britain* to Greek Line, *Empress of England* to Shaw Savill and *Empress of Canada* to Carnival Cruise Lines. It is now with considerable regret that I look back at those early days of Carnival and wish that I had made the effort to cross the Atlantic and take one of the cruises out of Miami operated by *Mardi Gras* – as *Empress of Canada* had become. But back then, filled with all the presumption of youth, I was dismissive of the Carnival operation: still wanting to see the former Canadian Pacific flagship sailing on long and luxurious cruises rather than on seven-day Caribbean jaunts. Perhaps, like many others, I did not realise that *Mardi Gras* was then the very spearhead of a cruising revolution.

When visiting friends in Liverpool in the mid-1970s, I found a souvenir ashtray from *Empress of England*. Styled to resemble a ship's wheel, it has a brass centre and within that an enamelled medallion showing the less-than-attractive green company logo and the legend 'CP Ships *Empress of England*'. My friends had cruised aboard her and talked of her with great affection. Sadly, it was to be the nearest I got to that particular 'White Empress'.

It was not until early 1999 that a chance comment to a friend suddenly prompted us to book a cruise aboard the former *Empress of Britain*, by that time sailing as *Topaz*. I feel a special affection for this ship as we share the same birthday, albeit that she is seven years younger than I. That apart, the former *Empress of Britain* does exude a very special atmosphere of warmth and friendliness. It is an atmosphere that lured me back for a longer cruise, three years later.

I was one of the lucky passengers to be aboard the former *Empress of Canada* when she sailed as *Apollon* from Liverpool during 1999. There was a lot of enthusiasm for the return of the ship to her former home. It was therefore very disappointing that, as a result of boardroom politics, she was withdrawn.

By chance, *Empress of Canada* and *Empress of Britain* would, because of their rôles as the first ships of Carnival Cruise Lines, become two of the most significant liners ever built. It is just disappointing that *Empress of England* was not also able to enjoy an equally lengthy and successful career as her sisters.

Clive Harvey,
March, 2004.

Acknowledgements

So many people have been extremely helpful, kind and generous to me during the time that I have been writing this book. They have shared with me anecdotes and information, photographs and publicity material. Those special people are Kevin M. Anthoney, Hall Coons, Luís Miguel Correia, John D. Elliott, Roger Emtage, Ann Glen, Kevin Griffin, Andy Hernandez, Michael Hipler, George R. James, the late Diane Kolyer, Peter Knego, Chris Mason, Tony Mills, Steven Moore, Bruce Peter and Wilhelm Wimmer.

Very special thanks must go to Captain Stephen J. Card for having created such an evocative painting for the front cover; to Peter C. Kohler, who shares my enthusiasm for those wonderful 'Empresses', for kindly writing the Foreword; and to Anthony Cooke (Mr. Carmania Press) for having accepted the project and for making it a reality.

Bibliography

Books:
Frank O. Braynard & William H. Miller: *Fifty Famous Liners, Vol. 3*, Patrick Stephens, Ltd.
Nicholas T. Caris: *North Atlantic Passenger Liners Since 1900*, Ian Allan, Ltd.
Philip Dawson: *Cruise Ships: An Evolution in Design*, Conway Maritime Press.
Bob Dickinson & Andy Vladimir: *Selling the Sea*, John Wiley & Sons, Inc.
Maurizio Eliseo: *The Sitmar Liners & the V. Ships*, Carmania Press.
Clive Harvey: *The Saxonia Sisters*, Carmania Press.
Brian Ingpen & Robert Pabst: *Maritime South Africa: A Pictorial History*, Jane's Publishing Co., Ltd.
Richard de Kerbrech: *Shaw Savill & Albion: The Post War Fortunes of a Shipping Line*, Conway Maritime Press.
Arnold Kludas: *Great Passenger Ships of the World*, Patrick Stephens, Ltd. and Koehlers Verlaggesellschaft, GmbH.
William H. Miller: *Ocean Liner Chronicles*, Carmania Press.
William H. Miller: *The Cruise Ships*, Conway Maritime Press.
William H. Miller: *The Last Atlantic Liners*, Conway Maritime Press.
William H. Miller: *Picture History of British Ocean Liners, 1900 to the Present*, Dover Publications.
W. H. Mitchell & L. A. Sawyer: *Cruising Ships*, Macdonald & Co. (Publishers), Ltd.
George Musk: *Canadian Pacific: The Story of a Famous Shipping Line*, David & Charles.
Peter Plowman: *Emigrant Ships to Luxury Liners*, New South Wales University Press.
John Townsend Gibbons: *Palaces That Went to Sea*, Nereus Publishing Company.
Robert Turner: *The Pacific Empresses*, Sono Nis Press.

Newspapers, magazines and periodicals:
Cruising & Cruise Ships (Luís Miguel Correia article 'The Last Empress Liners').
Fairplay Cruise Ship Review, 1987 (Laurence Miller article 'From the Golden Fleet to the Fun Ships').
Globe and Mail, The (Toronto).
Journal of Commerce, The.
Liverpool Daily Post, The.
Lloyd's List.
Marine Engineer & Naval Architect, The.
Montreal Star, The.
Sea Breezes.
Sea Lines, the magazine of the Ocean Liner Society.
Shipbuilder & Marine Engineer, The.
Ships Monthly.
Shipping & Transport.
Shipping World, The.
Shipping World & Shipbuilder, The.
Steamboat Bill, the journal of The Steamship Historical Society of America.
Syren and Shipping Illustrated, The.
Via Port of New York.

Foreword

By Peter Kohler

My first ocean liner book was Gordon Newall's *Ocean Liners of the 20th Century*. Forty years ago, you could count on the fingers of one hand the newly-published volumes on what was still a vital and active form of transportation. Today, when the ocean liner is as dead as a dodo, a dozen or so new ship books appear annually. Amid this burgeoning biography, occasionally there comes an especially welcome work about the ships and the routes that have, for no good reason, been denied their due.

White Empresses is just such a book. It is remarkable that so few books have been written on what was once the greatest travel system in the World. Canadian Pacific truly spanned the globe with trains, hotels, an airline and ships: coastal, cargo, trans-Pacific and trans-Atlantic. For many, it was hard to envisage a trip that did not include more than a fleeting glimpse of the CP beaver or, towards the end, that crazy circle in a square 'thingy' that was called, only by those who conjured it up, the 'Multimark'. It's the beaver that most people remember. A symbol of Canada every bit as much as the Maple Leaf. In a very real sense, CP bound the Dominion together with ribands of steel in a way it had not been before the trans-continental railway. But CP was more than trains. As *The Last White Empresses* reminds us, it was ships.

If the Canadian Pacific railways bound Canada together, CP ships – the 'Monts', the 'Duchesses' and the 'Empresses' – welded the Dominion into the Imperial communication chain. The creation of the 'All Red Route' at the turn of the century coincided with the apogee of the British Empire. And it rather cleverly put Canada at the nexus of Imperial transportation. One could travel from Liverpool to Hong Kong without ever having to endure 'foreigners' and 'queer lingoes' and all the time one would eat off the same china pattern and silver. It was a remarkable progress across two oceans and a mighty continent. A delightful progression from trans-Atlantic 'Empress' from Liverpool to Montreal; to trans-continental train with stopovers in some of CP's peerless 'chateau' hotels in Banff or Lake Louise; to trans-Pacific 'Empress' from Vancouver to Hong Kong or Yokohama.

The Last White Empresses is a poignant bookend to the story of CP passenger ships, rather than the ambitious beginning or the heyday of the 'Empresses' between the Wars, when *Empress of Japan* (1930) and *Empress of Britain* (1931) were icons of the Ocean Liner Era. Clive Harvey has a rather more challenging, but no less rewarding, task in bringing us, for the first time, the comprehensive story of the final trio of 'Empress' liners. Even if not born amid Depression or challenged in war, *Empress of Britain* (1956), *Empress of England* (1957) and *Empress of Canada* (1961) had, if anything, even more demanded of them – conceived in the turbulent post-War era and facing the new and ultimately irresistible aviation age.

Uniquely at the time, CP embraced this new era, consigning the fabled trans-Pacific route to its own fleet of airborne 'Empresses', while concentrating its trans-Atlantic focus on what had always been its bread-and-butter trade: the emigrants and the middle class tourists. The days of *Empress of Britain* girding the World for 120 days were over. But this new post-War fleet of CP ships still had a vital rôle to play as Canada beckoned to a new wave of immigrants and a newly buoyant tourist trade. Considering that CP had practically invented comfortable and affordable trans-Atlantic travel with its development of 'Cabin Class' steamers just prior to the First World War, this final trio of 'Empress' liners was far more in keeping with CP's roots than the lavish pre-War *Empress of Britain*.

The story of the final 'Empresses' is a fascinating and complex one. Admirably designed, staunchly built and ideal for the changed post-War world, they were always more interesting and innovative than their nearest competitors, Cunard's *Saxonia* quartet, which Clive Harvey has already chronicled in a previous Carmania Press volume. It is worth recalling that in such changed circumstances, these three 'Empresses' were in very select company. Only Cunard's *Caronia* (1949) was larger among the new post-War British North Atlantic liners. The CP trio intrigue with their mix of external innovation, as British architects discovered the sublime curves of streamlining, and internal pre-War Ocean Liner Odeon. The culmination of this synthesis of trendy and traditional was the magnificent *Empress of Canada* of 1961, surely one of the finest looking liners of her age.

Even more intriguing are their post-CP careers and *Empress of Britain* and *Empress of Canada* went on to play a critical rôle as *Carnivale* and *Mardi Gras* in the foundation of what is, indisputably, the greatest cruise ship operation of them all, Carnival.

Clive Harvey and I were awkwardly 'introduced' some 23 years ago, when our respective letters were published in a well-known British maritime monthly under the wrong names. Clive never wrote a better letter than the one I penned on *Uganda*! We went on to a frequent and fulsome correspondence that led to the first of many regular meetings. Later, we were both aboard the Polish *Stefan Batory*'s first Norwegian fjords cruise. She was then, of course, the last liner on the Canadian run and as such carried on some of the CP traditions. That led us to muse, rather too publicly it appears, how wonderful it would be if Polish Ocean Lines were to acquire *Mardi Gras*, ex-*Empress of Canada*, as a too perfect replacement for the ageing *Stefan Batory*. We were both bemused to find our fantasy printed shortly thereafter in a book as a real live 'rumour'! Sad to say, it was not a rumour, let alone a fact. Sadder still, it is now a pipe dream never to be realised.

As I pen this, the former *Empress of Canada* is en route to the breakers at Alang, India. Thus passes the last classic British trans-Atlantic liner in anything like her original condition. With her goes a lot of maritime history. And, ironically, more so, not for being the last of the 'Empresses' but as the first of the Carnival Cruise Line 'Fun Ship' fleet. As such, she will always be remembered as the start of a new era, rather than the end of an old one. Thirty-two years ago, no one could have believed that the somewhat faded ex-'Empress' stuck on a Miami sandbar would begin a fleet that would eclipse even the great Canadian Pacific at its heyday.

Immaculate in buff and white, streamlined profile silhouetted against the soot-stained Liver Building, our 'Empress' liner gently rises and falls in the Mersey, impatiently pulling against the creaking wooden planks of Prince's Landing Stage. Embark now on a voyage not only from Mersey Bar to Montreal but back to a not too long ago era when Canadian Pacific 'Spanned The Globe'.

Peter C. Kohler.

The *Empress of Japan* of 1891 was one of the first of the elegant 'Empresses'. She was a product of the Naval Construction & Armament Co, whose successors Vickers-Armstrongs built the final 'Empress' 70 years later. *Author's collection.*

1

The Early Empresses

"Sail to Europe through 1,000 miles of historic Canada. Magnificent White Empresses, sailing weekly between Montreal and Europe, offer the trans-Atlantic traveller a whole new world of luxury afloat. Spacious staterooms, the very finest cuisine and entertainment facilities are yours to enjoy. What better way to sail than along the sheltered St. Lawrence where a White Empress crossing takes you past 1,000 miles of ever-changing French-Canadian scenery. During the winter cruise season, a completely air-conditioned White Empress ship follows the trade winds to the colorful West Indies and South American ports of call. On the high seas with sleek White Empress luxury liners, as on land with stainless-steel dome streamliners and high in the sky with giant jet-prop airliners, Canadian Pacific offers a world of unsurpassed transportation service!"

These were the words that accompanied an evocative advertisement for Canadian Pacific in The National Geographic Magazine in the 1950s. The company advertised itself as "The World's Most Complete Transportation System", and truly it was. In the inter-War years it was possible to travel from Liverpool to Shanghai via Canada, without ever leaving the caring hands of Canadian Pacific. One of their White Empress liners would take you across the Atlantic and up the St. Lawrence River to either Quebec or Montreal. There, after a stay in a Canadian Pacific-owned hotel, you would board one of their trains to Vancouver, perhaps having stopped off at other Canadian Pacific hotels en route: at the Chateau Lake Louise, for example. Then, having arrived at Vancouver, you would board another gleaming White Empress, which would transport you across the Pacific.

After the Second World War, Canadian Pacific did not resume their trans-Pacific liner operations. Instead, you could soon journey almost two-thirds around the World by their own airline, which could now take you from Madrid or Amsterdam to Buenos Aires, Santiago and Lima; or down to Fiji, Auckland: or to Hawaii, Hong Kong or Tokyo. There was, of course, still the famous Canadian Pacific Railway, stretching all the way across the Dominion from Halifax to Vancouver. The company's chain of splendid hotels, from the baronial Chateau Frontenac and the Banff Springs to the Royal York in Toronto, the largest hotel in the British Commonwealth, also stretched across the country. Rounding out this enormous transportation company were their fleets of trucks and coastal ships. However, it was probably for their superb ocean liners that Canadian Pacific became so well known on both sides of the Atlantic.

While the ocean services began in 1887, it was earlier, on the 16th February, 1881, that the Canadian Pacific Railway Company was incorporated with the aim of building a line across the North American continent. Three months later, the work was begun but it was only after 4½ years of perseverance and hard labour that it was completed. The ceremony of driving home the final spike,

performed by Lord Strathcona, took place on the 7th November, 1885, marking the start of a new era for Canada. The birth of what would become a mighty steamship line occurred during the construction of the railway, when it became clear that a means of servicing the building of that section of the line which would run along the north shore of Lake Superior had to be provided. Supplies had to be arranged for the large number of men involved in the work. A contract was therefore placed on the Clyde for three steamers of about 2,800 tons. The *Algoma*, *Alberta* and *Athabasca* made the journey across the Atlantic under their own power. But as they were too large to get through the locks of the St. Lawrence and Welland Canals, they had to be cut into sections at Montreal and then towed to Buffalo, where they were put together again. It was in 1884 that they inaugurated the Canadian Pacific Railway's Great Lakes service but, sadly, it was to be an all-too-short career for the *Algoma*, which sank during a heavy gale on Lake Superior the following November. Her sister ships went on to give the company long service, however, and it was only in 1946 that they were disposed of.

Although the first through train left Montreal the day after the driving of the last spike, the actual service did not really begin until the 28th June, 1886. The distance between Montreal and the then western terminal, Port Moody at the head of the Burrard Inlet, was covered in 5½ days.

Canadian Pacific had already decided in principal to start a steamship service across the Pacific Ocean. In 1887, they chartered three ships for a route between Vancouver and the Orient. The *Abyssinia*, *Batavia* and *Parthia* were all former Cunard liners which had been sailing for the Guion Line. (Remarkably, one of them, the *Parthia*, remained afloat until the mid-1950s, although by that time relegated to service as a timber barge.) However, these three liners were little more than stopgaps for Canadian Pacific. In 1889, the company signed an agreement with the Post Office to carry mail. The contract included a time clause, which specified that the vessels to be used in the service should have the capability of making 17½ knots, and 16 knots on a 400-mile sea trial, as well as satisfying Admiralty requirements should they be needed for use as armed merchant cruisers. Clearly, new ships were an essential requirement.

The company gave the work of constructing the first 'Empress' ships – three elegant forerunners to the final and equally elegant 'Empresses' – to the Naval Construction and Armament Company of Barrow-in-Furness, which would go on to play a further significant part in the future of Canadian Pacific. These shipbuilders already had a fine reputation and this was further enhanced when the three magnificent clipper-stemmed steamers, *Empress of China*, *Empress of India* and *Empress of Japan*, entered service in 1891.

These three original 'Empresses' were sister ships with

two funnels and three masts and were propelled by a twin-screw installation of triple-expansion machinery. Built of steel, they had a gross tonnage of 5,920 and were 485 feet long and 51 feet wide. They had accommodation for 180 passengers in First Class, 32 in Second Class and 600 in Steerage. In addition, there was a capacity for 3,250 tons of cargo. All the very latest improvements in ocean travel were embodied in their construction and the cabins and public rooms – in First Class at least – were luxuriously furnished, well ventilated and lighted by electricity. The three ships cost approximately £200,000 each to build. On the measured mile and on the 400-mile sea trials, they all exceeded their guaranteed speed.

As the new 'Empresses' neared completion, Canadian Pacific advertised inexpensive round-the-World trips, starting with the delivery voyages calling at Gibraltar, Naples, Port Said, Suez, Colombo, Penang, Singapore, Hong Kong, Woosung, Nagasaki, Kobe and Yokohama. Passengers would stay on board for the first sailing from there to Vancouver and would then cross Canada by train. Finally, they would return to Britain by any line of steamships – all for £120. All the berths were soon booked and the first of the sisters to make the voyage was the *Empress of India*. At anchor in the Mersey prior to her departure, she attracted much attention on account of her fine lines and white hull.

Empress of India's passage out east was in the nature of a running-in period and she steamed to Hong Kong at little more than half speed, arriving there on the 23rd March, 1891. She left Yokohama on the 17th April on the last leg of the voyage and, although she met with heavy weather, she reached Vancouver on the 28th, having made a trans-Pacific passage in 10 days 14 hours 34 minutes, at an average speed of 17 knots. A fast special train then carried passengers and mails to Montreal. The overall journey time from Yokohama to Montreal was 14 days 22 hours. This was later surpassed by the *Empress of Japan*, which left Liverpool on the 11th April, 1891. The final ship of the trio, *Empress of China*, was given a rousing send-off as she left Liverpool three months later, on the 15th July, to join her sisters in the Pacific.

In 1896, Canadian Pacific purchased more lake and river steamers. By this time a further branch of the railway had been extended and important mining districts were added to the overall sphere of the company's operations. The Klondyke gold rush of 1897 prompted the purchase of the Union Line steamers *Tartar* and *Athenian*. *Tartar* left Southampton on the 8th February, 1898 with a full cargo of provisions, camping and mining equipment and the first of the British adventurers on their way to the gold fields. The *Athenian* followed soon afterwards. After the gold rush, the two ships were placed in a secondary Pacific service.

It was by now becoming increasingly obvious to the company that the time was ripe for them to develop a trans-Atlantic service. A major step in this direction was made in March, 1903 with the acquisition of the fifteen ships of the Beaver Line, which ran services to Canada from Liverpool, Avonmouth and London. In 1904, the London service was extended to include Antwerp. The appearance of Canadian Pacific on the Atlantic intensified the rivalry which had existed between the Beaver Line and the Allan Line and, with a view to strengthening its position on the Canadian route and in order to maintain its mail contract, the Allan Line ordered two new liners. Canadian Pacific met the challenge by placing an order with the Fairfield Shipbuilding & Engineering Company, Ltd. of Glasgow for two twin-screw, twin-funnelled, 14,190 gross ton ships which would be the pioneer Atlantic 'Empresses' – the *Empress of Britain* and the *Empress of Ireland*. With a contract speed of 19½ knots, they were more than a match for the Allan liners and they brought nearer the realisation of the "20 knots to Canada" project that Canadian business people had been advocating for some time.

A plan by Allan Line to build two 18,000-ton liners was shelved owing to prohibitive costs and, instead, the two 11,000-ton ships *Grampian* and *Corsican* were placed on the service. Even then, there were signs of compromise in the operations of the Allan and Canadian Pacific fleets and Allan's *Victorian* and *Virginian* were having to share the mail contract with the two 'Empresses'. Indeed, this tendency to compromise would eventually lead to the amalgamation of the two companies.

Canadian Pacific met a major setback on the 26th July, 1911 when the *Empress of China* was wrecked at Yokohama. It was also at this time that, in order to counter the competition from the heavily subsidised Japanese company Toyo Kishen Kaisha, Canadian Pacific placed an order for another pair of liners from the Fairfield company, the *Empress of Russia* and the *Empress of Asia*. Of 16,900 gross tons, they were the first British liners to be built with cruiser sterns. Their 20-knot speed, high-class accommodation and general design were such that they had no difficulty in restoring the Red Ensign to its pre-eminent position in the trans-Pacific trade. The Atlantic service suffered a serious loss, however, when, on the 29th May, 1914, the *Empress of Ireland* sank after a collision with the Norwegian collier *Sorstad* off Father Point in the St. Lawrence. 1,024 lives were lost.

With the outbreak of the First World War, nearly all of the company's ocean-going ships were pressed into the service of the national interest. In all, during those years of conflict the Canadian Pacific fleet carried over one million troops and passengers as well as four million tons of cargo and munitions. The losses in ships and men were considerable but the performance of services so vital to the War did not cease. On the 19th January, 1916, the amalgamation of Canadian Pacific and Allan Line was announced and sixteen Allan ships were transferred to the Canadian Pacific flag. A number of these became war losses and in the following years several of the older Allan ships were sent to the breakers.

Losses in passenger tonnage had to be made up and, in order to meet the situation until new ships could be built, four former German liners were bought from the Shipping Controller: *Kaiserin Auguste Victoria*, which became the *Empress of Scotland*; the *Tirpitz*, which was initially called *Empress of China* and then, in 1922, *Empress of Australia*; the more modestly sized *König Friedrich August*, which was renamed *Montreal*; and the *Prinz Friedrich Wilhelm*, which became the *Montlaurier*. The first of the post-War liners to be completed were the *Montcalm* and the *Montrose*, delivered by John Brown and Fairfields respectively in December, 1921 and March, 1922. The third of this trio of 'Monts' was the *Montclare*, also built by John Brown and delivered in August, 1922.

The John Brown shipyard also built three of what were

to become the highly acclaimed 'Duchess' liners for the company. The first of these, the *Duchess of Bedford*, entered service in May, 1928 and that December the *Duchess of Richmond* was delivered, followed by the *Duchess of York* in March, 1929. The second ship of the quartet, *Duchess of Atholl*, had been built by William Beardmore & Co. and was handed over to Canadian Pacific in June, 1928.

In June, 1930, the splendid 26,032 gross ton *Empress of Japan* joined the fleet. Another product of Fairfield Shipbuilding & Engineering, she was Canadian Pacific's largest and most beautifully appointed liner. However, while undoubtedly the star of the company's Pacific fleet, she was perhaps a little overshadowed the following year by the entry into service of a new Atlantic liner, the *Empress of Britain*. Built by John Brown, she was at 42,348 gross tons the largest passenger ship to come from a British yard since the White Star Line's *Britannic* of 1915. The magnificent, three-funnelled *Empress of Britain* was sumptuously furnished and ranked along with the great ships of state more commonly found on the New York route. She acquired an enviable reputation for her long

wintertime cruises, which took her around the World. Unfortunately, her career was to be brief. On the 26th October, 1942, she was bombed while 70 miles north west of Ireland and, while great efforts were made to get her safely to port, she was an easy target and was destroyed by torpedoes from a German submarine. *Empress of Asia*, *Empress of Canada*, *Duchess of York* and *Duchess of Atholl* would also fall victim to enemy action in the Second World War.

After the War, the first new ships to join the Canadian Pacific fleet were seven 'Beaver' class cargo liners. In addition, in September, 1947 the company purchased the 9,034-ton cargo-passenger vessel *Huascaran* from the Canadian War Reparations Committee. She had originally been owned by the Hamburg Amerika Line and Canadian Pacific renamed her *Beaverbrae*. The prestigious former *Empress of Japan*, whose name had been changed to *Empress of Scotland* during the War, did not return to her original Pacific route but now strengthened the depleted Atlantic fleet. The *Duchess of Richmond* was renamed *Empress of Canada* but, while undergoing some refitting

The famous 1931 *Empress of Britain* was arguably the most luxurious British liner ever built. She was also the largest passenger ship ever owned by Canadian Pacific. *Author's collection.*

work in Liverpool's Gladstone Dock in January, 1953, she was destroyed by fire. The refit had been in anticipation of an increase in trans-Atlantic business due to the Coronation later that year and, in fact, the *Empress of Canada*'s sailings were already heavily booked. Canadian Pacific were therefore anxious to replace her as quickly as possible and in March they acquired the 18,435 gross ton *De Grasse* from the French Line and renamed her *Empress of Australia*. She had the distinction of being the first single-funnelled 'Empress'. With her somewhat modest speed of just 16 knots, she was out-classed by her fleetmates and was always considered to be little more than a stopgap. In April, 1956, with the advent of the third *Empress of Britain*, she became surplus to the company's requirements and was sold.

Such was the progress of Canadian Pacific's shipping interests. As the *Empress of Britain*, the twenty-first ship to be built for the Canadian Pacific Railway by the Fairfield Shipbuilding & Engineering Co., Ltd., was being prepared for her maiden voyage, her sister, *Empress of England*, was being readied for launching. And, on a wave of confidence and optimism for the future of ocean travel, Canadian Pacific were already beginning to discuss placing tenders for a third new ship. She would, of course, emerge in 1961 as the *Empress of Canada*. No one could have realised it at the time, but these fine liners would be the last three 'White Empresses'.

The new *Empress of Britain* on her launch day, 22nd June 1955, at Fairfield's yard at Govan.
A. Ernest Glen. Bruce Peter collection.

2

The new *Empress of Britain*

The April, 1954 issue of *The Marine Engineer and Naval Architect* reported that on the 9th March Canadian Pacific Steamships, Ltd. had placed an order with Vickers-Armstrongs, Ltd.'s Walker-on-Tyne yard for a 22,500 tons gross, 21 knot passenger and cargo steamship for their trans-Atlantic services. The liner would be the largest to have been built on the Tyne since 1939 and it was anticipated that she would join the Canadian Pacific fleet in early 1957. The report went on to say that she would be the second of two sister ships, the first of which was already under construction by the Fairfield Shipbuilding & Engineering Co., Ltd. at Govan. She would cost more than $15,000,000, being one of the largest dollar orders to be received by a British company at that time. She would be entering service in the early Spring of 1956 and would be named *Empress of Britain*. She would introduce a 'new look' to the company's fleet.

The Canadian Pacific Railway's Annual Report for 1945 had stated that "the resumption of service on both the Atlantic and the Pacific is the immediate aim of your directors." Plans were prepared for two large new passenger ships, one for the Atlantic and one for the Pacific. However, it was clear that it would be several years before full services could be resumed and it was decided that, at least for the time being, efforts would have to be concentrated on the Atlantic. As a result, the three remaining liners were placed onto the Atlantic service as soon as they were reconditioned.

Following the tragic loss of *Empress of Canada* in 1953, the Canadian Pacific fleet was made up of five 'Beaver' cargo vessels, all dating from the mid-1940s; the *Maplecove* and *Mapledell*, both former 'Beavers'; and the trans-Atlantic passenger liners *Empress of France* (ex-*Duchess of Bedford*), dating from 1928, *Empress of Scotland* (ex-*Empress of Japan*) of 1930 and the 1924-built *Empress of Australia*. The ageing passenger ships were facing increased competition.

As early as 1951, the Cunard Steam Ship Co., Ltd., Canadian Pacific's great rival on the Liverpool – St. Lawrence route, announced their intention to build a new class of passenger liners for the Canadian trade. The initial announcement stated that there would be just two ships but later this was expanded to four. In November, 1953, just seven months after Canadian Pacific had found it necessary to purchase the twenty-nine year old former *De Grasse* to supplement their magnificent but elderly duo of liners, Cunard announced that the first two of their new ships would be named *Saxonia* and *Ivernia*. They were already under construction, with *Saxonia* scheduled for launching in just three months time. The mighty Canadian Pacific was faced with the very real need to meet the Cunard challenge in order to maintain a viable presence on the route.

It was, however, not just a case of competing with the new Cunard liners. The whole concept of ocean liner transportation across the Atlantic was changing: more people could now afford to travel and, in that first decade after the end of the Second World War, there were also many migrants looking to begin new lives in North America. The Holland America Line had been one of the first companies to recognise this change and to respond to it by offering simple but attractive, comfortable and affordable Tourist Class accommodation. In 1951 and 1952, they introduced the twin 15,000-ton liners, *Ryndam* and *Maasdam* into their New York service with occasional calls at Canadian ports. (In 1960, a more regular Canadian service was started.) Although they did not at first compete directly with the Canadian Pacific ships, the *Ryndam* and *Maasdam* caused a minor sensation on the North Atlantic, being primarily geared towards the transport of Tourist Class passengers. They each had accommodation for approximately 850 in that class and only a token 39 in First Class, necessary in order to conform to the regulations of the North Atlantic Conference.

Likewise, Cunard's new *Saxonia* and *Ivernia* were also geared strongly in the same direction, with over 800 in Tourist Class and 110 in First. Their subsequent sister ships would also emerge with a strong bias towards Tourist Class, although with 100 less in that class and about 50 more in First. Canadian Pacific's *Empress of France* and *Empress of Scotland*, though totally refurbished after the War, represented another age and were distinctly First Class liners. The *Empress of France* could carry 400 in First and 300 in Tourist Class, while the *Empress of Scotland* accommodated up to 458 in First and a mere 250 in Tourist. It was only the recently acquired stopgap, *Empress of Australia*, which reflected the new trend with her 220 First Class passengers and 444 in Tourist Class. (That was probably more due to the fact that as French Line's *De Grasse* she had never been one of the 'glamour ships' of the Atlantic but somewhat in the 'second league', rather than any forward thinking on the part of Canadian Pacific.)

It was therefore quite understandable that Canadian Pacific had taken a most cautious approach towards replacing their Atlantic passenger fleet and did not place an order until the first new Cunarder had entered service. The 'new look' to the company's fleet referred to in the press reports was also a reflection of the 'new look' on the Atlantic. The new Cunard liners were undeniably handsome; nevertheless, there was still a very traditional air about them, both internally and externally. There is no doubt that Canadian Pacific paid very close attention to the design of the *Saxonia* before placing the order for the new ship which would become their *Empress of Britain*.

A considerable amount of scientific and experimental research work was carried out at the National Physical Laboratory before the designs were completed, aimed at determining not only the most efficient hull form but also at reducing both rolling and pitching as much as possible.

In addition, the superstructure and the funnel were aerodynamically tested in the wind tunnel. In appearance, the *Empress of Britain* would differ substantially from any other liner of a similar class then sailing and particular attention was given during the design stages not only to her outside appearance but also to her internal arrangements. Every effort was made to subordinate many of the functional features, traditional in ship design and which could not be removed, so that they would harmonise with modern trends, while at the same time preserving a well-balanced ship appearance. Special attention was given to the design of the rudder to ensure manoeuvrability at low speeds, in view of the necessity for good handling while navigating the St. Lawrence. Steering tests were carried out with a model in a tank and very good manoeuvrability was achieved at a speed of just 5½ knots.

The accommodation and services for the passengers were given the greatest possible attention and the architect responsible made a close study of many arrangements in good hotels in both America and Canada and combined these with what was regarded as 'the best British practice'. Thus, even before *Empress of Britain* had emerged from her builders' yard, she was being regarded as spacious, well-lighted and comfortably furnished.

The year 1955 was most significant for Canadian Pacific. On the 11th January, the first keel plates of the *Empress of England* were laid at the Vickers-Armstrong (Shipbuilders), Ltd. yard at Walker-on-Tyne. Six months later, on Wednesday, the 22nd June, over 10,000 employees of the Fairfield Shipbuilding & Engineering Co., Ltd. gathered along with their families to watch Her Majesty Queen Elizabeth, accompanied by the Duke of Edinburgh, launch the *Empress of Britain*. Just before she stepped up onto the launching platform, the Queen was presented with a bouquet by the Hon. Robert Bruce, the 2 year-old grandson of Lord Elgin and Kincardine, chairman of the Fairfield company. Once on the launch platform, she took the specially carved mallet and with it released the mechanism which set in motion the hull of the new 'Empress'. To the cheers of the assembled crowd, the newest Canadian Pacific liner entered the water for the first time.

On that day, a young woman, Ann Glen, accompanied her father, A. Ernest Glen, to watch the launching from the opposite bank of the river:

"I was eager to see a big ship launched and this liner would be just about as big as it was possible to slide into the narrow waters of the Upper Clyde. This waterway is really a man-made canal where the original wide, shallow and meandering river has been straightened, deepened and inevitably narrowed by engineering exertions over many decades.

"As my father had once worked for the Clyde Navigation Trust as a Resident Engineer when King George V Dock was being constructed in the latter 1920s, he had got to know the river very well. This was especially valuable when it came to seeking out vantage points for such events as launches. From Kelvinbridge we took the Subway to Merkland Street and then walked to Merkland Wharf. My father had previously found out that the launch would take place in the early afternoon when there would be a good high tide. I was warned to stand well back from the edge of the quay as the displacement of water in the narrow waterway might spill over the margin – father had

seen people who had ventured too near the launch ways get a soaking, if not being washed right off their feet.

"So we looked across the river to Fairfields, where the new liner *TS Empress of Britain* (yard number 731) towered above the stocks, awaiting launching by Her Majesty, The Queen. The hull was pristine white. Flags were flying. Tugs, both Clyde Shipping Company and Steele & Bennie varieties, were fussing about. Various banging and crashing noises came from the yard at intervals. 'They're taking out the last of the blocks holding the hull in place,' said my father. He pointed out the Clyde Trust vessel, *Clyde*, and the River Police patrol boats. A crowd gathered around us – dock workers and others who were just curious to see what was going on. Of course, no shipping movements were allowed on the river for some time before and after a launch. There was no wind and, although it was overcast, the light was quite bright.

"After about half an hour, we could hear bands playing, and it was the National Anthem. Then we could hear – thanks to the loud speakers and the carrying power of water – a girlish voice say in precise tones: 'I name this ship *Empress of Britain*. May God speed her and all who sail in her.' There were cheers from the yard and then, ever so slowly, the hull of the new ship began to move down the ways. Father explained that these had been amply greased. Meanwhile, he was busy with his camera and records. 'The launching speed rapidly increases, the cradle collapses and the stern submerges deeply, setting up a great wave,' he told me. This wall of water surged across the river and, thankfully, spent itself on the wall of the wharf without overtopping it.

"But still the ship came on and got remarkably close. The drag chains had produced clouds of dust and rust. When the new 'Empress' stopped, the tugs quickly manoeuvred, ropes were thrown and they took charge. Those at the liner's stern were the *Flying Petrel* and *Chieftain*. Then, *Strongbow* came on the scene as the 'Empress' was towed clear of the timber wreckage floating on the surface. The tugs slewed the liner straight in midstream.

"By now, we could see the launching platform, which was decked out in red, white and blue, and we could just make out in the distance a small figure in a pastel outfit clutching a bouquet. 'That must be the Queen,' said someone. 'She's no' the wan wi' a bowler hat, ony way,' joked another.

"In a combined effort, the tugs were intent on getting the *Empress of Britain* safely into the Fairfield fitting out basin, which was just a little down river, but adjacent to the launching site. The tug *Cruiser* had joined the fray and slowly the liner was eased into the basin, bow first. We watched until the last of the tugs had left, the Police launches had gone and the debris from the launching had been cleared up....."

As the team of tugs manoeuvred the new 'Empress', the Queen and the Duke of Edinburgh took tea in the joiners' shop, which overnight had been transformed into a flower-decked reception room. Later, the Royal party saw a series of mock-ups of First Class and Tourist Class passenger cabins and an exhibition of tinted water colour drawings of the public rooms, which had been executed by A. M. McInnes, Gardner & Partners, the decorators of the ship. Lord Elgin afterwards presented the Queen with a casket containing two 17th century silver tankards and six

Her Majesty Queen Elizabeth II launched the second *Empress of Britain* **on the 22nd June, 1955 from the Fairfield company's yard at Govan. In these rare pictures taken by an onlooker, we see the ship entering the waters of the Clyde.** *A. Ernest Glen. Bruce Peter collection.*

Now afloat, the uncompleted ship is marshalled towards the fitting out basin by the tug *Flying Merlin*. Both vessels are dressed overall.
Laurence Dunn collection.

contemporary silver bon-bon dishes, for use aboard the Royal Yacht *Britannia*.

In her speech accepting the gift, the Queen said: "I know how keen an interest this splendid new ship is arousing both in Canada and here. In her we welcome the forging of a further link between my peoples on either side of the Atlantic." Her Majesty said that the new liner replaced the famous Canadian Pacific of the same name, launched by the Prince of Wales in 1930 and later lost by enemy action. "We can be sure that, like her predecessor, the new *Empress of Britain* will write a notable page in the story of ocean travel." She went on to say that she felt sure that Fairfield's had never built a finer ship and added that she knew that everyone who had a hand, great or small, in her design and construction would share the pride that she felt in their work.

The *Empress of Britain* had the proud distinction of being the first Canadian Pacific liner, and the first Fairfield-built vessel, to have been named by a reigning sovereign.

The following day, *The Journal of Commerce and*

Watched by proud shipyard workers, the new 'Empress' lies in the Clyde, which is littered with débris from the launch. *Laurence Dunn collection.*

Shipping reported: "The visit yesterday of Her Majesty the Queen, Master of the Merchant Navy and Fishing Fleets, to the Govan shipyard of Fairfield Shipbuilding & Engineering Co., Ltd. to perform the naming ceremony of the launch of the liner *Empress of Britain* provides another instance of the continuing interest which the Royal Family takes in the country's shipping industry. Yesterday's launch marked the second occasion on which Her Majesty has launched a ship since her accession to the Throne, the previous instance being on the 17th August, 1954, when she visited Belfast, there to name the Shaw, Savill liner *Southern Cross*. It is thus the more regrettable that yesterday's ceremony should have taken place at a time when industrial unrest – evidenced in the unofficial strike of a very small section of seafarers – should be disturbing the hitherto harmonious relations in the shipping industry. Fortunately, there seems to be every indication that this ill-advised strike is on the wane and that the liners whose sailings have been cancelled will shortly be maintaining normal sailings on the North Atlantic – a service in which the great ship launched yesterday will in due time be called upon to play her part."

The *Journal of Commerce and Shipping* went on to remind its readers that *Empress of Britain* was the third ship to bear that name, each of them having been Clyde-built. The first had been the 15,800-ton Fairfield-built vessel of 1906; and the second had been the company's magnificent 42,350-tonner which came from Clydebank in 1931. It went on to make a most interesting observation that the 26,000 gross ton size of the new liner was indicative of the approach towards the 'mammoth' liner between the wars as compared with the present policy of building smaller passenger ships, dictated to some extent by the high cost of new tonnage and competition from the air. In a further lengthy article, the paper went on to speculate whether the future of the big passenger liners might lie with the gas-turbine as their means of propulsion.

At the time of the launching of the *Empress of Britain*, many of the great shipping companies were still concentrating on rebuilding their fleets after the devastating effects of the War. Shipping lines, and particularly those employed in the North Atlantic trade, were about to experience a renaissance and the threat of competition from the air was not particularly considered by most of them. Canadian Pacific, however, were by this time also in the airline business. They had acquired several small carriers in Canada during the 1940s and in 1942 had set up Canadian Pacific Airlines Limited. By 1949, with the shipping side of the business focussed on the Atlantic, the airline was in a position to take over where the Pacific liners had ruled supreme before the War. So, Canadian Pacific had perhaps a clearer idea than most of what the future might hold.

On the 28th October, 1955, just four months after the launching of *Empress of Britain*, the headline: "Large British Jet Liner Needed" appeared in *The Journal of Commerce and Shipping*. The article went on to celebrate: "Cheering news that Britain is going to have an airscrew-turbine transport, the Rolls-Royce-engined Vickers Vanguard, available for operation in the early 1960s and designed to meet the traffic requirements of ten years hence, as far as it can be seen now. Since that good news, it has been announced that Canadian Pacific Airlines has placed an order for three Bristol Britannia 300LR

airscrew-turbine air liners and has taken an option on a further five – the first Commonwealth airline order for the Britannia." The age of the trans-ocean airliner was slowly dawning.

However, at this same time it was reported that in the first nine months of 1955, 20,640 more passengers crossed the Atlantic by sea rather than in the corresponding period of the previous year. A statement made by the North Atlantic Conference said that ships operated by member lines carried 18,464 more passengers from the United States and Canada than in the January to September period of 1954, and 2,176 more passengers from Europe. Although the proportion of total trans-Atlantic passenger traffic carried by air had increased from 31.56 per cent in 1950 to 38.12 per cent in 1954, there were many signs of confidence among the shipping companies that for another 'ship life', if not longer, the sea route would succeed in attracting sufficient numbers of passengers to remain viable. Indeed, there were several significant liners under construction. As the *Empress of Britain* neared completion in the Fairfield yard's fitting out berth, Swan, Hunter & Wigham Richardson on the River Tyne were getting ready to deliver the Norwegian America liner *Bergensfjord*. Meanwhile, Italy's Ansaldo yard was completing the *Gripsholm* for the Swedish American Line and *Statendam* was in the early stages of construction at the Wilton Fijenoord shipyard for Holland America. Apart from the new Canadian Pacific liner, there were seven Atlantic passenger ships due for completion before 1960, totalling 175,000 gross tons – at that time a remarkable figure.

On the 29th February, 1956, having moved from her berth at the Govan yard to carry out preliminary trials, the *Empress of Britain* was caught by a sudden squall. She swung broadside, striking the quay wall of the King George V Dock and also the stern of the tanker *British Sportsman*. It was a minor incident causing only slight damage to some port plates of the new liner but it followed a couple of other incidents. There had been two small fires, one on B Deck aft on the 25th October, 1955 and one on the 13th December in the engine room caused by a fault in the electric wiring. However, both fires had been quickly extinguished before the arrival of the fire service and neither caused damage of any consequence. They did not unduly affect the progress of fitting out and, in fact, the liner was completed ahead of schedule. Having left the Fairfield yard, the new 'Empress' departed from the Clyde on the 1st March for the River Mersey and entered the Gladstone Dock the following day. While there, she was given an underwater inspection and underwent cleaning and painting before being returned to the Clyde on the 8th to carry out her speed trials.

After anchoring overnight at Lamlash, she ran her main speed and endurance trials off the coast of Arran Island over the next two days. These completed, *Empress of Britain* spent nearly three weeks in the King George V Dock in Glasgow and during this time was visited by thousands of Fairfield workers along with their friends and families, youth organisations connected with the sea and guests of the builders. At noon on Thursday, the 29th March, 1956, under the command of Captain S. W. Keay, the new ship made her second journey down the Clyde, this time to carry out some minor trials in deep water before the flag of Canadian Pacific Steamships. Ltd. replaced that of her builders. The handing over ceremony

The new *Empress of Britain* makes a spectacular sight as she turns at speed during her trials.
Luis Miguel Correia collection.

took place that evening while the ship was at anchor off the Tail of Bank. It was a particularly notable occasion because it was being held two days before the date specified in the contract, which had been signed on the 18th November, 1952. A newspaper commented that her early delivery was an achievement to put against the complaints then common about the shipbuilding industry's failures to meet delivery dates.

The early morning arrival of the *Empress of Britain* off Liverpool created much interest and comment. Only a few days before, it had been reported that the venerable 1917-built troopship *Lancashire* was to be withdrawn from service and had already been sold for scrap. The announcement of the demise of this elegant survivor of the First World War era aroused considerable passion and the Liverpool-based *Journal of Commerce and Shipping*, on reporting the arrival of the new Canadian Pacific ship,

could not help but make comparisons between the two vessels:

"... yet even though this gulf of years lies between them, both ships seem to have one thing in common – that indefinable beauty of line which one poet was once to sum up – 'these famous ships, each with her grace and story'. Although very definitely of her generation, the *Lancashire*, with her three tall masts and pencil slim funnel and long hull compared with her beam, is a very elegant and trim lady of whom it can be said with regret that her like will never be seen again. Indeed, there are many seafaring men and those whose interest lies in ships who, if asked to choose between the two ships in the matter of hull design, would undoubtedly champion the older one. That is not to admit that the modern passenger liners as represented by this latest *Empress of Britain* have not a dignity that is peculiarly their own. But it must be confessed that they all appear to be stamped in the same mould. The product of the naval architect and marine engineer of today, they are sea-going examples of the post-war tendency to reduce everything to a common denominator. Indeed, as one elderly observer was heard to remark yesterday, 'When you've seen one you've seen the lot!'.".

The *Empress of Britain* did, however, present a fine profile with her seemingly low superstructure, gracefully tiered after decks and stepped forward decks. It was certainly, as promised in those early press releases, an entirely 'new look' and a very modern look for a trans-Atlantic liner. In fact, no other liner would appear on that ocean with such a radical profile as the *Empress of Britain* and *Empress of England* until Holland America's magnificent *Rotterdam* of 1959.

Before starting her maiden voyage to Montreal, the *Empress of Britain* was scheduled to make a 'shake-down' cruise to Southampton with 400 guests of the line on board. Her departure from Liverpool on the 9th April was a most exciting moment for the port, for, as the *Empress of Britain* moved into the river and headed out towards the sea, the even newer *Reina del Mar*, arriving from her sea trials, made her way towards the dock. Thus, the World's two newest liners, prime examples of British shipbuilding, were in Liverpool at the same moment.

The coastal voyage from Liverpool to Southampton was, by all accounts, most enjoyable. It was as if the weather sought to prove itself no less agreeable than the ship. She made a steady passage at between 20 and 22 knots and only by a couple or so of minor rolls could her passengers, mostly still in their cabins at the time, detect that she was 'rounding the corner' off South West Cornwall. Captain Keay said that she handled beautifully but added that there had been no occasion to use her stabilisers – except to test them. He had served on the previous *Empress of Britain* and had been aboard her when she was attacked and sunk in the War. In an interview with the Press, he said that he did not think that the size of the new 'Empress' was likely to be greatly exceeded in the future. While off Fawley, making her way into

Southampton, she was saluted by the troopship *Empire Ken*, which mustered her men at Boat Stations and dipped her ensign. Then, as she passed the Ocean Terminal, the *Queen Elizabeth* blasted a salute on her siren. The new ship, the first 'Empress liner' to visit the port for over two years, docked at Berth 101 in the New Docks. The buildings were decorated with flags and bunting and a large banner reading 'Welcome – Good Luck, *Empress of Britain*'.

She really did differ considerably in her appearance from any other liner then in service, not only externally but internally as well. Indeed, one shipping journalist described her as 'Britain's most interesting ship of the decade.' The fact that she was the first completely air-conditioned passenger vessel to be built in Britain was in itself enough to make her a noteworthy liner. For both First and Tourist Class passengers there was a modern permanent cinema and also a swimming pool and a spacious ballroom/lounge. Other rooms included a library, a writing room, lounges, smoking rooms, cocktail bars and children's playrooms. The First Class passengers also enjoyed a Sun Verandah-Lounge with a glazed roof and glass doors, which opened out to a sheltered Sun Deck situated between two blocks of officers' accommodation up on the Boat Deck.

The newspaper *Lloyd's List* reported on her arrival in Southampton that she would undoubtedly prove to be one of the most popular liners crossing the Atlantic. "For comfort and real quality in ship decoration and furnishing – indeed, luxury in many respects – the new flagship sets a new standard in North Atlantic travel. This applies particularly to Tourist Class. *Empress of Britain* is primarily a Tourist Class ship. The distinction between the two classes is almost negligible and the generous Tourist public rooms, to say nothing of most of the cabins, are in literal truth first class. Throughout the ship, the decorators have combined merit and restraint. She is in every respect modern, yet allied with that modernism is a pleasing conservatism, which results in a happy effect of harmony and comfort. All tastes have been catered for and minor

The strikingly modern profile of the new liner aroused much comment, not all of it entirely favourable.
Luís Miguel Correia collection.

points have not been overlooked. For instance, every cabin is fitted with a point for the greatly increased use by men of electric shavers. For her size, *Empress of Britain* is probably one of the most expensive ships yet built in this country, costing something in the neighbourhood of £6½ million."

Free of cargo-handling machinery, ventilators and other such obstacles, and with flush-fitting hatch covers, the amount of open deck space available for passengers was a very special feature of the ship. Although essentially a passenger liner, *Empress of Britain* also had space for the carriage of approximately 3,000 tons of cargo, including a large amount of refrigerated space for fruit and other Canadian produce. The hatchways to the cargo spaces were large and the 'tween deck was especially high so that cars could be garaged there.

Bearing in mind that, for at least part of the year, the ship would encounter ice conditions in the St.Lawrence River, her hull was suitably strengthened. In addition to the keel, the sheer strake and two strakes of plating above the waterline were of special quality welding steel and the scantlings of the frames and the shell forward were increased for ice stiffening. All butts were welded and there were only four riveted seams on each side, while the frames in all cases were riveted. All the decks, with the exception of the Promenade and Boat Decks, were welded. There were seven decks in all: Boat and Promenade; and then A, B, C, D and E. The ship was sub-divided below Deck C by eleven watertight bulkheads; and above that by six main fireproof divisions, giving seven fireproof zones.

While the previous *Empress of Britain* had been renowned for her sumptuous interiors, decorated by the likes of Sir Frank Brangwyn, Sir Charles Allom, Sir John Lavery and Edmund Dulac, and was quite the equal of the great 'ships of state', her post-War successor established a new era and a new style for Canadian Pacific. This new style was all the more evident when compared to that of her fleet-mates. In many respects, they were similar to liners built shortly before the First World War, while the new ship fully reflected modern tastes and styles.

The most significant change to greet passengers was the fact that the Tourist Class accommodation had been upgraded beyond recognition, whereas First Class public rooms seemed much smaller (and indeed they were). Reproductions of past periods in furniture and other decorations had completely disappeared, except in one instance where a modified Regency-styled room served as some consolation to traditionalist tastes. Among the public rooms, the one that caused most comment was the Empress Room, which was available to both First and Tourist Class passengers. In those much more 'class-conscious' days, such a concept was an innovation and one report commented in somewhat condescending tones; "This has much in its favour, for it is not uncommon for a First Class passenger to find that he has one or two friends travelling Tourist and vice versa: and the Tourist passenger seldom feels happy about visiting the First Class accommodation, nor does the First Class passenger relish paying a visit to the Tourist accommodation. In the Empress Room, however, they may meet on neutral ground, without any of the formalities required by the ship's officers before a passenger may cross a barrier between one class and another. Apart from this aspect,

however, many arguments can be advanced in favour of a social centre for all passengers irrespective of class. But should any passenger, First or Tourist, prefer to keep to his own class, the *Empress of Britain* provides ample accommodation for reading, writing and social activities in both parts of the ship."

The Empress Room, situated on the Promenade Deck, was beautifully decorated. Most of its floor area was carpeted. To either side, it had bow windows hung with floor-length drapes of cherry velour. A handsome metal balustrade with a gilt finish separated the raised outer seating area from the central, circular dance floor. The room had been very cleverly designed so as to appear neither square nor oblong and, to enhance this effect, the aft bulkheads that framed the Tourist Class entrance were curved. These bulkheads were most handsome in that they were panelled in a golden shaded material known as Warerite. These panels were inset with vignettes designed by the artist Margot Cragg which showed a variety of subjects: a figure with an umbrella walking a dog; a castle on top of a precipice; a thatched cottage; a policeman directing traffic. Their small size, however, made them difficult to appreciate in such a location.

Forward of the Empress Room were the two main First Class public rooms: the Drawing Room and the Club Room, which in total occupied almost as much deck space as the Empress Room but were divided by a gently curved bulkhead running across the ship. The Drawing Room, according to publicity material at the time, 'paid tribute to the Regency period'. However, given its grey and burgundy abstract floral design carpet, coupled with yellow brocade-covered chairs, it was difficult to appreciate the Regency theme the designer of the room was aiming for. The Club Room had as its main feature a bar front decorated in maroon leather and trimmed with bands of gilt metal. The room was panelled in olive ash veneers and was decorated with a collection of sporting prints by the Canadian artist Archibald Forbes. There were also four bas relief panels depicting the seasons. Wrapping around the Club Room, and giving a view forward, was the Garden Lounge. Altogether, First Class passengers enjoyed a very elegant and modern suite of rooms.

From the main entrance and enclosed promenade, stairs led up to the First Class Sun Deck, Sun Lounge and Promenade Deck. The Sun Lounge was designed with the feel of a penthouse in mind, with full-height windows reaching from deck to deckhead and sloping backwards in true penthouse fashion. These windows were designed to be opened wide in good weather, thereby giving access directly onto the sheltered Sun Deck – a feature which was probably more appreciated when the ship was cruising than when she was crossing the North Atlantic. The room was decorated with small panels by the artist Joyce P. Collins, depicting objects associated with the sea and ships: a compass, ship's lantern, figurehead, anchor, etc.

Aft of the shared Empress Room on the Promenade Deck were the Tourist Class public rooms: Smoking Room, Lounge, Cinema, Library and Writing Room. A report at the time described them as being "equipped in a sumptuous manner for this class of travel". The floor of the Smoking Room was covered in a rubber material coloured to look like stone paving and deep pile rugs were laid on top of it. On the starboard side of this room was the

The First Class Restaurant and the Tourist Class Cocktail Lounge showed a refreshing modernity, unusual in a British liner of the time. *Bruce Peter collection.*

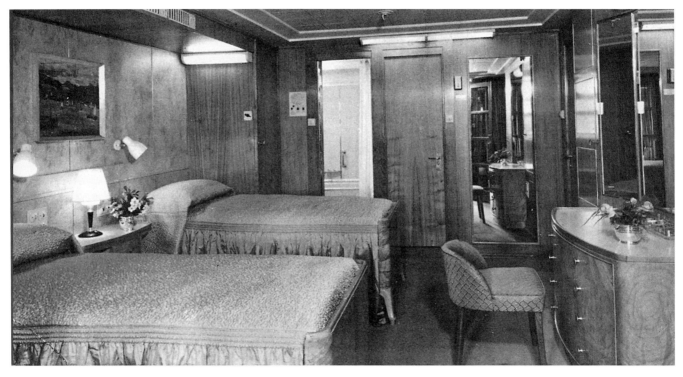

Although predominantly a Tourist Class ship, *Empress of Britain* also had extremely well-appointed First Class accommodation, such as this double stateroom. *Author's collection.*

Cocktail Bar – a rather small space considering the number of Tourist Class passengers. It was, however, attractively furnished and decorated, with a dramatically patterned carpet and with the walls covered in murals by J. A. Coleman. The chief feature of the room, though, was a deep and wide mural on the after wall, by Warwick London. In this, the artist had contrived magnificently to combine the decorative with the informative - the coats of arms of the ten provinces of Canada in heraldic colours appeared against the Dominion's wide open spaces and the Atlantic and Pacific Oceans, with the outlines of Western Europe on one side and the Pacific islands on the

other. In addition, it depicted the Canadian Pacific empire: its ocean liner, railroad and airline routes as well as the company hotels.

Further aft, through glazed doors, was the Tourist Class Lounge. This was attractively panelled in white sycamore relieved at intervals by burr veneers. The principal decorative features were a series of dramatic floral studies, again by Warwick London. Aft of the Lounge, on the port side, was the Tourist Class Writing Room and in the corresponding space on the starboard side was the most attractive Library. Here was a desk from which the library steward issued the books and bookcases with gilt metal grilles, while the bulkheads were panelled in decorative veneers. In the Writing Room there were desks topped with green leather, for 18 passengers, and the panelling was in avoudire and burr veneer.

On C Deck, three decks below the principal run of public rooms, were the two Dining Rooms, with galleys between. These maintained the same decorative style as the Lounges and a reporter visiting the ship commented: "How pleasant to find a luxurious pile carpet beneath one's feet! This merits special mention for in so many instances the passengers travelling British must tolerate an unfriendly deck of linoleum or rubber, a carpeted deck being usual in ships foreign-owned or foreign-managed." The First Class Dining Room stretched just two-thirds the way across the ship from the starboard side. The main decorative feature was a series of murals by C. Cameron Baillie, depicting some of Canada's most colourful

A four-berth stateroom with shower, one of the small number of Tourist Class cabins to have private facilities. *Author's collection.*

flowers and birds. Cut glass panels and mirrors gave added interest, dividing the room into smaller sections so that groups of people could dine with a feeling of some intimacy yet were not deprived of the spaciousness and splendour of the room as a whole.

Whilst the reporter had waxed lyrical with regard to the carpet in the First Class Dining Room, he let pass the fact that the equivalent Tourist Class room was a sea of autumn-hued linoleum. It was nevertheless a handsome room, its bulkheads being panelled in Canadian maple, burr walnut and African elm. 'Lively interest' was added by several murals by R. D. M. Robertson, some of which were mounted on the boiler trunking and acquired a three-dimensional quality by being reflected in mirrored panels fixed to the ship's side. An unusual feature of the room were the raised sections or alcoves, with balustrades of gilt-metal and panels decorated with copies of ancient engravings of Liverpool and Quebec – the panels being encased in a synthetic resin to protect them.

A swimming pool, available to both classes, was located on D Deck in a position beneath the First Class Dining Room.

As we have seen, *Empress of Britain*, followed the new trend of being principally a Tourist Class ship, with accommodation for 900 passengers in that class and just 150 in First. A and B were the principal accommodation decks, although there were some cabins on C Deck, forward of the First Class Dining Room and a small number aft of the Tourist Class Dining Room. Both First and Tourist Class passengers boarded the ship at A Deck in adjoining Entrance Halls, divided by the Purser's Bureau. The central part of this deck was given over to the First Class cabins, all of them with private bathrooms. Twenty-four of these cabins, twelve on each side, were designed to be converted into two-, three- or four-room suites. Forward of the Entrance Halls and also in the aft quarter of the deck were two blocks of Tourist Class cabins, all of which were provided with private showers and toilets. However, none of the Tourist cabins on either B or C Decks had private facilities. Although she was designed very much with the Tourist Class passengers in mind, the *Empress of Britain* still provided a very exclusive and special experience for those travelling in First Class.

There was a hospital located aft on B Deck. Crew accommodation was mainly on D Deck, although there was also some aft on both B and C Decks as well. Captain's, Officers' and crew accommodation was of a high standard. There were complete suites of rooms for the Captain, Chief Engineer and Staff Commander, with furniture made of specially chosen woods. All other officers had single-berth cabins equipped to the same standard as those for the passengers.

Although the *Empress of Britain* was rich in highly polished wood veneers throughout her public rooms and cabins, approximately 100,000 sq. feet of Warerite decorative laminated plastics were also used in her fitting out – for murals, wall panels, ceilings and table tops. At the time, this was one of the largest contracts for this material in a ship of this size. For protection against fire, the ship was fitted out in excess of the requirements of the day. In addition to being sub-divided into fireproof zones, she was equipped with an automatic sprinkler and alarm system in the passenger accommodation. Not only did the wheelhouse act as a fire control station but there were two

others, one forward and one aft, situated at the crew gangways. Each was complete with electric alarms, telephones, CO_2 detecting equipment and automatic sprinklers and was capable of being kept in constant touch with any part of the ship.

About 110,000 sq. feet of the fire retardant material Marinite was also used. One of the blocks of Tourist Class cabins forward on A Deck was constructed of it, occupying all the space between two 'A' class divisions. The cinema was also lined with Marinite for additional safety. Furthermore, the hygienic properties of the material were employed to advantage in the sheathing and ceiling of the main galley. All 'A' class divisions and stairwells were also insulated with Marinite.

A considerable number of tests were carried out by Canadian Pacific to study the effects of various kinds of lighting on the appearance of both make-up and clothing. As a result, the General Electric Company supplied 3,719 yards of cold cathode tubes giving either an ivory or a gold light. As a result of the publicity surrounding these tests, the *Empress of Britain* was sometimes referred to as 'the Ladies' Ship'.

The reporter who had covered the new liner for *The Journal of Commerce* finished his report by stating: "Swimming pool, children's playrooms and Garden Lounge continue the fresh appeal and up-to-date equipment, the attractive colour balance and the careful study of passenger comfort so outstanding in all other sections of this new ship, which cannot fail to bring prestige to her owners, to the craftsmen who built and equipped her and to the decorative artists who designed the public apartments."

The main propelling machinery and boilers were constructed at the works of the Fairfield Shipbuilding & Engineering Co. and incorporated the latest improvements in high-speed turbine and water-tube boiler practice. There were two sets of Fairfield-Pametrada double-reduction geared turbines designed for a combined output of 27,000 s.h.p. at service speed and 30,000 s.h.p. at maximum speed. Each set consisted of an h.p. and i.p. turbine in tandem and an l.p. turbine, driving their own pinions at 4,195 r.p.m. and 3,452 r.p.m. respectively. There were two Foster Wheeler controlled superheat boilers and one Foster Wheeler reheat boiler. Each was arranged with a superheater, economiser and steam air heater. Each boiler was served with a Howden forced draught fan and an induced draught fan.

At 26,000 gross tons, 640 feet in length, 85 feet in width and with a draft of 29 feet, the new 'Empress' liner was a little larger than her Cunard rivals. She presented a more modern profile – it was stated at the time that she was arguably the finest-looking post-War liner built on the Clyde, or indeed in the rest of the World. While decorated in up-to-the-minute styling, she was not as controversial as the *Saxonia* and *Ivernia*, nor did she resort to the melange of period styles affected by the *Carinthia*. She was designed with future use as a cruise ship in mind and this was emphasised by her attractive livery of white hull and upper works with a green sheer-line at C Deck level. Her funnel was more yellow than buff and bore the Canadian Pacific red and white chequerboard motif. It has been claimed that the *Empress of Britain* set standards of naval architecture which became the norm for future shipbuilders throughout the World. Certainly, she was the

Empress of Britain **manoeuvres in the port of Montreal. Immediately behind her funnel can be seen one of the freighters of the rival Donaldson Line.** *Laurence Dunn collection.*

best-looking vessel to have been produced by the Govan yard.

Empress of Britain had arrived in Southampton at the end of her shakedown cruise on the 10th April, 1956. She sailed back to Liverpool on the following day, with another party of invited guests and was then made ready for her maiden voyage to Canada. After the final cleaning, fine-tuning, loading of cargo and stores, she embarked her passengers on the 20th April and, dressed overall, sailed out of the Mersey. Five days later, she arrived in Quebec and reached Montreal on the 26th, remaining there until the 1st May, when she departed on her return voyage to Liverpool.

Her early months were not without incident: her second voyage to Canada was a stormy one and she sustained some weather damage. Then in June and July, she suffered some machinery problems, which resulted in the need for repairs to a generator. These were, however, all relatively minor and the new 'Empress' settled well into

her regular schedule of trans-Atlantic crossings, the port of St. John, New Brunswick being substituted for Quebec and Montreal between November and March, when the St. Lawrence was impassable due to the winter ice.

After barely five months of service, *Empress of Britain* again made the news – and in glorious fashion. At the time, there was rivalry between Canadian Pacific and Home Lines, whose *Homeric* was running to the St. Lawrence from Southampton. Home Lines had proudly announced that *Homeric* had made an eastbound crossing from Quebec to Le Havre in 4 days 23 hours and 25 minutes, at an average speed of 22.02 knots, the fastest post-War sailing on the route. The *Empress of Britain*, as the new Queen of the Canadian service, could obviously not allow the 24-year old *Homeric* to steal her glory and she responded accordingly. On the 11th September, 1956, Canadian Pacific announced that when she berthed at Liverpool the previous day, she had broken both the eastbound and westbound times between Liverpool Bar

Light and Father Point, Quebec. She had crossed from Liverpool to Father Point in 4 days 17 hours and 42 minutes, an average speed of 21.43 knots, reducing her previous time by 12 minutes. The return voyage took 4 days 18 hours and 48 minutes, an average speed of 21.26 knots, which reduced her previous eastbound time by 59 minutes. She had thus made a briefer, though not faster, voyage than the *Homeric*. A few weeks later, on the 5th October, she suffered some damage to her hull plates when high winds caused her to hit a concrete wall as she was leaving Liverpool's Gladstone Dock for the Prince's Landing Stage where she was due to embark her passengers.

She continued sailing to Quebec and Montreal during that first year of service through until late November; then, on the 7th December, she departed Liverpool on her first voyage to St. John. She made three further voyages to that port during the deepest winter months, on the second of which, the 1st January sailing, she created some media attention: she was carrying over 500 Hungarian refugees. The 1st January was an auspicious date for them to start a new life. On the 18th January, *Empress of Britain* arrived back in Liverpool nine hours late, having experienced some problems with her port engine as she was approaching the Mersey. Tugs were called to assist her for the final 20 miles to the port. However, only a minor adjustment to the engine was required. That first season of winter voyages ended when she arrived in Liverpool on the 5th March. She remained there until early April, undergoing overhaul and routine maintenance work. During this time, on the 9th March, she suffered slight damage when a fire broke out in one of her D Deck cabins.

Although primarily a trans-Atlantic liner, *Empress of Britain* was built with cruising also in mind. Here she is at Lisbon on the 27th February, 1962. *Luís Miguel Correia collection.*

Sunlight and shadows show up the welded and riveted construction of *Empress of England* as she lies at the fitting out quay at Vickers-Armstrongs' Naval Yard on the Tyne. *Laurence Dunn collection.*

3

Empress of England

Canadian Pacific were in a state of high excitement in early May, 1956: the *Empress of Britain* had returned to Liverpool at the end of her successful maiden voyage and on the 9th May, Lady Eden, the wife of the Prime Minister, was to perform the naming ceremony of the *Empress of Britain*'s sister ship, *Empress of England*. The Managing Director of Canadian Pacific Steamships, Mr. A. C. Macdonald, had crossed on the *Empress of Britain* to attend the ceremony. When he arrived at Liverpool, he told waiting reporters that tenders for yet another 'Empress' liner, to replace the 26 year-old *Empress of Scotland*, would be sought from both British and foreign shipyards later in the year. The company hoped that if they did proceed with their plans, the new liner would be ready for service by the Spring of 1960. "Whether or not we actually build a new passenger vessel depends largely on delivery dates, price consideration and the terms of the tender received," said Mr.Macdonald.

Several days earlier, in his address to shareholders at the Annual General Meeting held in Montreal, Mr. N. R. Crump, the President of the parent Canadian Pacific Railway, had said that a formidable problem was presented by the high cost of ship construction. He estimated that at 1956 prices, it would cost $50 million to replace the company's eight ships. He noted that *Empress of France* would be disposed of at the time of the entry into service of *Empress of England* and that there was also a possibility of replacing *Empress of Scotland*. "Active consideration is being given to the construction for this purpose of a third new ship," said Mr. Crump. "She would probably be of greater tonnage than either 'Britain' or 'England' and with design and appointments to make her particularly suited to cruise requirements as well as North Atlantic service." It was expected that this potential new ship would cost approximately £7,850,000.

The launching of *Empress of England* on the 9th May, was a particularly exciting event: it was the first time that Canadian Pacific had used this name for one of their liners and it was therefore appropriate that she should have been constructed in an English shipyard. Also, quite apart from the expected 10,000 spectators in the Vickers-Armstrongs yard at Walker-on-Tyne and the thousands lining the opposite bank of the river, the launch was broadcast on the BBC's Home Service and was also filmed for later showing on both the BBC and ITV television services. The BBC created a documentary film about the liner, entitled *Tomorrow She Sails*, and this was transmitted on the eve of her maiden voyage.

During the latter stages of her fitting out, a strike seemed inevitable which threatened the total closedown of the country's shipyards from noon on the 16th March, 1957, the day she was scheduled to leave the yard. The shipbuilding unions approached the National Union of Seamen, asking them to restrain their members from taking the newly completed *Empress of England* out on her trials: she was due out of the yard only half an hour after the strike was due to start. Nevertheless, the liner left on schedule: the builders had taken the precaution of handing her over to Canadian Pacific before she sailed and she was thus technically no longer in their hands.

As *Empress of England* moved down the Tyne, led by the tug *George V*, she gave a farewell blast on her siren. The trials were held in the Firth of Clyde off the Isle of Arran, with the Canadian Pacific officers under the direction of Vickers personnel. As a result of a re-arrangement of the trials programme, it was not until the 25th March that the new liner left the River Clyde and she made her first arrival in the port of Liverpool the following day, rather than on the 22nd as had at first been planned. She remained there until the 18th April, when she left on her maiden voyage to Canada, just two days short of the first anniversary of the initial departure of *Empress of Britain*. Aboard were 158 First Class and 900 Tourist Class passengers. Dressed overall, the new ship, with her white hull, green hull line and buff funnel with its chequered house flag marking, looked a worthy addition to Britain's merchant fleet. Shortly before the liner left the Mersey, Captain C. L. de H. Bell, her Master, sent a message to Lady Eden. He referred to the *Empress of England* as "this fine vessel" and asked Lady Eden to pass on to her husband, Sir Anthony, the wishes of both the passengers and crew for his speedy recovery to good health.

In all major respects, the *Empress of England* was identical to the *Empress of Britain*, though there were some differences in the arrangement of the windows below the bridge wings and in the layout of the public rooms and decoration. At the time of the *Empress of England*'s entry into service, the journal *The Shipping World and Shipbuilder* wrote: "Externally, the *Empress of England* is an extremely close sister of the *Empress of Britain*. These ships have a modern and attractive appearance, though the large funnel is somewhat gaunt. For classic elegance of line and balance of silhouette, the Scandinavians are, of course, unbeatable: their trans-Atlantic liners look like yachts. But the two new 'Empresses' give an impression of greater size than the latest Scandinavian liners and their appearance has perhaps more character."

Empress of England carried eight more passengers in First Class than her sister, giving 1,058 in all, divided into 158 in First Class and 900 in Tourist Class. Her crew numbered 464. She had six holds, arranged three forward and three aft. They provided a total of 380,650 cubic feet of cargo space, of which 80,000 was refrigerated. The forward holds were all ahead of the bridge, thereby allowing unrestricted open deck space for passengers aft of the bridge and keeping the cargo working arrangements clear of the passenger spaces as far as was possible. As on her sister ship, Number 2 hatch was exceptionally large, to allow cars to be loaded. All the hatches were served by 5-ton derricks, with the exception of Number 2 where a 10-ton derrick was fitted.

The aerodynamically shaped 'fireman's helmet' funnel casing, constructed of aluminium alloy and weighing 56 tons, is lowered into place. *Laurence Dunn collection.*

In layout and decoration of the passenger spaces, *Empress of England* followed closely the design of her sister. One or two alterations had been made, however, no doubt in the light of experience. The First Class restaurant, for instance, was a little larger. A further alteration was made to the First Class Drawing Room and to the adjacent Club Room: whereas on *Empress of Britain* the wall dividing these two spaces was curved, on *Empress of England* a more conventional, straight wall separated the two rooms. The scheme of decoration was very similar on the two ships, modern in style without being in any way Contemporary. Overall, the effect was very attractive. *The Shipping World and Shipbuilder* commented: "If a criticism is to be made, it is that while this general style is most effective for Tourist Class accommodation, it is not always so happy in the First Class public rooms, where an effort is usually made to heighten the effect of luxury by the use of richer and more highly patterned fabrics and carpets, which do not always agree with the clean and simple lines of the furniture and general décor."

By confining the boiler and engine room uptakes to a comparatively large number of correspondingly small trunks, it was possible to create public rooms extending the full width of the ship amidships. As with the '*Britain*', in addition to the swimming pool and cinema, the two classes shared one of the principal public rooms, again called the Empress Room. The passenger cabins also followed the principles set down by *Empress of Britain*: First Class staterooms all on A Deck amidships, and all with private bathrooms. They were panelled, using three basic schemes with variations between the woods used for the walls and for the furniture. Tourist Class staterooms

were situated on A, B and C Decks, those on A Deck all having shower and toilet. The cabins were for two and four people, the latter having two upper folding berths. Decoration was based on five different schemes: paint was used in pastel shades matching the plastic panels lining the undersides of the folding upper berths and the wall around the large wash basin with which each room was provided. The accommodation for the crew was of the same high standard as that aboard the earlier ship.

Empress of England, like her sister, was fitted with eight 36-foot Fleming gear hand-propelled lifeboats, each having a capacity of 146 people, also one 36 foot Class A motor lifeboat accommodating 132 persons and one Class B motor lifeboat that could also carry 132, both being powered by Thornycroft engines. In addition, there were two 26-foot emergency boats fitted with Fleming hand-propelling gear and with room for 46 people. All the lifeboats were of Birmabright alloy and were manufactured

In this advertisement extolling the merits of the new *Empress of England*, Vickers-Armstrongs boast of receiving the order for the next 'Empress' liner.
Author's collection.

International Design and Equipment, 1958   105

Empress of England

This 25,500-ton liner, engaged on the trans-atlantic route with Canadian Pacific, is noted for her modern construction and design.

Echelon arrangement of decks, smoke eliminating funnel, and extensive lift installations, have been incorporated for their passenger appeal. Other features, such as special rudder design to ensure good manoeuvrability at low speed, and comprehensive radar systems, make her exceptionally easy to handle.

Vickers are proud of this latest 'White Empress' and of receiving the order to build the next new liner for the Canadian Pacific fleet.

VICKERS

VICKERS-ARMSTRONGS (SHIPBUILDERS) LIMITED · VICKERS HOUSE · BROADWAY · LONDON · SW1
TGA BT276

by Hugh McLean & Sons, Ltd. The davits were of the Welin-Maclachlan overhead gravity type and were capable of handling the larger boats with two-part tackle but in the case of the emergency boats using single part falls to facilitate rapid lowering and recovery.

The ship was also equipped with Denny-Brown stabilisers. It was anticipated that in rough weather these would reduce a roll of 18 degrees to one of less than 6 degrees. The machinery installation in *Empress of England* was of the same 30,000 s.h.p. steam turbines, working on the reheat system as developed by Fairfields and fitted aboard *Empress of Britain*.

Empress of England arrived at Quebec for the first time on the 25th April, 1957 and reached Montreal the following day. She departed from there on the 30th and was back in Liverpool on the 6th May, her maiden voyage successfully completed. The fine new twin liners were now set to maintain Canadian Pacific's presence on the North Atlantic.

On the 3rd July, the President of the Canadian Pacific Railway Company announced in Montreal that contract negotiations had been entered into with Messrs. Vickers-Armstrongs, Ltd. for the construction of a passenger liner for the Canadian Pacific Steamships, Ltd. of Liverpool. This, of course, was the contract that both he and the Managing Director of Canadian Pacific Steamships had alluded to at the time of *Empress of England*'s launching. The announcement went on to say that the contract was estimated to be valued in the region of £8,000,000. The hull was to be laid down at the Naval Yard, Walker-on-Tyne (where, it will be remembered, the *Empress of England* had been built) and the propelling machinery was

to be constructed at the firm's Barrow-in-Furness works. As anticipated, the new liner was to be larger than either of the two previous ships. She would have accommodation for approximately 200 First Class and 875 Tourist Class passengers. Like the two earlier ships, she was to be designed for the North Atlantic service in the St. Lawrence summer season and for cruising in the winter. To make her fully suited to these rôles, she would be completely air-conditioned and fitted with stabilisers and would have both indoor and outdoor swimming pools.

With the entry into service of *Empress of England*, the Canadian Pacific fleet briefly contained four liners: the two new ships plus their older fleetmates, *Empress of Scotland* and *Empress of France*. However, just prior to the launching of *Empress of England* it had been indicated that *Empress of France* would soon be withdrawn, while the *Empress of*

This photograph of *Empress of England* during her trials in the Firth of Clyde was taken while she was at anchor but, for publicity purposes, it was 'touched up' to give the impression that she was in motion.
Laurence Dunn collection.

Scotland would be retained until possibly replaced by a new ship in or around 1960. Nevertheless, in November, 1957 *Empress of Scotland* made her final voyage for the company. Later she would be sold to Deutsche Atlantik Line and would enter trans-Atlantic service for them as the considerably restyled *Hanseatic*.

The service to Canada at that time was dominated by Canadian Pacific and Cunard, both with fleets of principally new ships: within less than two months of *Empress of England* making her maiden voyage Cunard took delivery of *Sylvania*, the last of their quartet for the Canadian service. Among the other companies operating on the Northern Europe – St. Lawrence route was the Europe-Canada Line with a wartime-built former C3-type freighter which had been converted into the migrant carrier *Seven Seas*. Polish Ocean Lines entered the service in August, 1957 with their famous *Batory* and in May, 1958 Greek Line placed their newly-acquired *Arkadia* on the route. Home Lines had the 25,000 gross ton liner *Homeric* sailing to Quebec and Montreal and she would be briefly joined in 1959 by her fleetmate *Italia*. All of these

companies offered direct competition to both Cunard and Canadian Pacific: each of their ships included a call at Southampton in its itineraries and all were geared to carry principally Tourist Class passengers. The *Batory*, *Arkadia*, *Homeric* and *Italia* offered a high standard of service and accommodation but the Canadian Pacific and Cunard Lines had the advantage of having several ships on the route, enabling them to offer a very regular service. Thus, the other companies had to rely on passengers from other European countries to fill most of their berths.

Empress of Britain resumed sailings to the St. Lawrence on the 5th April, 1957 after overhaul and maintenance work. Having sailed on her homeward journey from Montreal on the 16th, she passed her new sister *Empress of England*, outward bound on her maiden voyage. On the *Empress of England*'s second voyage, while in the St. Lawrence in the vicinity of Father Point, she suffered an engine problem. On her arrival at Montreal, it was discovered that her port-side high-pressure turbine rotor was bent. It was removed and sent by air to the builders for repair. Meanwhile, temporary repairs were made to enable the ship to continue with her normal service. This did, though, slow her so that instead of reaching Liverpool on the 27th May, as scheduled, she arrived two days later, on the 29th. It was normal practice for the Canadian Pacific liners to have either a two- or three-day turn around: the time needed to unload and load cargo, as well as to prepare for the next lot of passengers. However, on this occasion she was made ready for her return voyage in barely 24 hours. She was in the news again on the 29th August, when she was in collision with the ore carrier *Sept Îles* at Quebec. Fortunately, neither ship was seriously damaged.

Whereas *Empress of Britain* maintained her regular trans-Atlantic service throughout the year, *Empress of England* was to become the company's cruise ship during the winter months. Having arrived back in Liverpool on the 2nd December, she was made ready to face the rigours of cruising the Caribbean rather than the storm-tossed Atlantic. The *Empress of Britain* was also in the Liverpool docks at that time, remaining there until early February. *Empress of England* sailed on the 3rd January, 1958 and called at St. John before continuing on down to make her first arrival at New York on the 13th January. Between the 15th January and the 28th March, she made just four cruises from New York. The first was of fourteen days, calling at Kingston, La Guaira, Curaçao, Cristobal and Havana. The second was of nineteen days with visits to St. Thomas, Grenada, La Guaira, Curaçao, Cristobal, Kingston, Port au Prince and Havana. The third cruise, also of nineteen days, had a similar itinerary but included Barbados. The final cruise was rather idyllic, being fourteen days long but calling at just three ports: St. Thomas, Cristobal and Havana.

After a two-day stay at New York, *Empress of England* sailed directly for Liverpool and, following a ten-day stopover during which she was made ready for the regular Atlantic service, she sailed for Quebec on the 18th April. Both sisters maintained a flawless, almost incident-free service during the Summer of 1958. *Empress of England*

did, however, suffer some minor fire damage on the 16th December, shortly after having been overhauled at Birkenhead. She was in the Gladstone Dock at the time, when overalls and rags, which had been left near an electric radiator in the elevator machine space on the port side of D Deck, started smouldering. The fire brigade was called but the damage was confined to a generator motor and some electric cables.

It was during 1958 that a change was introduced, first to the sailing schedules of *Empress of Britain*: on the 28th April, on her homeward voyage from Canada, she made her first call at Greenock. In order to reduce crossing times, this call had been dropped when she had been introduced. This had caused an outcry, both in Scotland and in Canada, and the Scottish Tourist Board had led a protest by many organisations, including Greenock Corporation. Hundreds of letters and telegrams were sent and the Secretary of State for Scotland was asked to lend his influence to the campaign to get the Clyde call reinstated. From that April onward, Greenock featured in most of her sailings to and from the St. Lawrence and the following April *Empress of England* also began to make regular calls at the Clyde port.

Once again, the *Empress of Britain* continued her regular Atlantic sailings throughout the winter months, with just four voyages being made to St. John between December, 1958 and March, 1959. By early April she was back on the Quebec and Montreal service. However, the effects of the winter were still being felt in the St. Lawrence. On the 11th April, while arriving from Liverpool, *Empress of Britain* suffered hull damage from ice in the river. Montreal had been cut off from the sea by an ice-jam 30 miles down river, near Sorel, less than a fortnight after the arrival of the first foreign vessel since the Spring thaw. This had delayed the sailing of the Polish *Batory* which had been due to sail for Europe with 600 passengers at dawn on the 12th. *Empress of Britain* was one of the last vessels, along with Cunard's *Carinthia*, to reach Montreal before the river became blocked. Meanwhile,

Looking immaculate, *Empress of England* lies at Liverpool, preparing to depart on her maiden voyage and showing off her shapely stern with its St. Lawrence anchor.
Laurence Dunn collection.

The Empress Room, shared by passengers of both classes, had an intriguing mix of decorative styles – Art Deco veneered panelling and chairs and carpets à la Festival of Britain. *Laurence Dunn collection.*

Jaunty maritime scenes decorated the walls of *Empress of England*'s smart, modern indoor swimming pool.
Author's collection.

Empress of England had operated a series of four cruises from New York to the Caribbean between the 14th January and the 27th March.

This pattern of service for the two ships came to a dramatic change in 1960. Inspired by the success of *Empress of England*'s winter cruise programme out of New York, the directors of Canadian Pacific had decided that it would be more profitable to operate both ships in this way rather than to maintain one of them on the often inhospitable Atlantic run during the depths of winter. At that time, Cunard were having difficulties trying to make a profit out of running their four new ships year-round on the Canadian service. However, with Canadian Pacific's rather more forward-thinking design, it was a relatively easy matter for the two 'Empresses' to adopt an off-season cruising rôle.

Both ships underwent refitting work at Liverpool prior to sailing for New York at the end of the 1959 Atlantic season. *Empress of Britain* arrived in Liverpool on the 8th December, joining *Empress of England* which had been there since the final day of November. *Empress of England* was the first to sail, departing for New York on the 2nd January, 1960 and arriving there on the 9th. *Empress of Britain* sailed out of the Mersey on the 6th but her voyage to New York was via St. John.

Each ship was scheduled to operate a programme of four cruises. *Empress of England*, having already acquired a reputation in American eyes as 'the' Canadian Pacific cruise ship, undertook the longer trips. The first was of fourteen days, while the others were of nineteen days duration. *Empress of Britain* operated one ten-day, one twelve-day and two fourteen-day cruises. The first departed New York on the 18th January and called at San Juan, Port au Prince and Nassau. The cruises were scheduled so that the sisters were never in the same port together, and neither did their arrivals and departures from New York coincide. The revolutionary turmoil in Cuba had made it off-limits to American tourists by this time, so sadly this once-exciting and popular destination was no longer featured amongst the exotic Caribbean ports of call. *Empress of Britain* arrived in New York at the end of her first series of cruises on the 14th March and

sailed for Liverpool two days later. Also after a two-day turn-around in New York, *Empress of England* sailed for Liverpool on the 30th March. Her voyage was via Greenock.

By mid-April, 1960, both ships were once again back into their routine of trans-Atlantic sailings to and from the St. Lawrence ports. Sadly, however, these became rather disrupted during the middle and later part of the summer: at the very height of the passenger-carrying season. Unofficial strike action had been afflicting many British ships for several months. The seamen were demanding a 44-hour week and a £4 per month pay increase. When *Empress of Britain* arrived in Liverpool on the 19th July, most of her crew members joined the strike. At what was reported to have been 'a stormy 40-minute meeting', more than 1,000 seamen from various ships voted to continue the strike action and there was every indication that it would go on until the end of the month. However, not all crews were supportive of the strike and the *Empress of France* was able to sail on the 21st, six days later than scheduled. Canadian Pacific announced that *Empress of Britain* would depart on the 22nd in accordance with her schedule. *Empress of England*, whose voyage had been cancelled at the start of the strike, was to remain in dock and then resume normal sailings the following week. Efforts to recruit a full crew for *Empress of Britain* succeeded and she cast of from the Prince's Landing Stage at mid-day, anchoring in the Mersey to await the arrival by special train from Glasgow of 200 passengers who should have boarded at Greenock. They embarked by tender and the liner sailed that night direct for Montreal, in order to maintain her schedule.

The labour unrest was not resolved, however, and when *Empress of Britain* arrived back in Liverpool on the 9th August, she became strike-bound along with many other vessels. Over 600 passengers were due to sail on her 12th August departure and the company made every effort to obtain sufficient crew to enable her to sail but, with shortages of personnel in all departments, the departure ultimately had to be cancelled. Arrangements were made with Canadian Pacific Airlines to transport those passengers who were willing to fly.

As usual, *Empress of England* arouses great interest as she docks at Montreal, with her cargo gear and her side ports already prepared for action. *Laurence Dunn collection.*

At a joint meeting of the crews of *Empress of England* and the Cunard *Carinthia* in Montreal, it was agreed that if the new conditions were unacceptable they also would join the strike. The dispute again brought the two Canadian Pacific sisters together: on her return to Liverpool on the 16th August, *Empress of England* joined the strikebound *Empress of Britain*. The '*England*' had been scheduled to sail for Canada on the 19th but this had to be cancelled, again with many passengers having to resort to aircraft to complete their journeys. Canadian Pacific had hoped that they would be able to send *Empress of England* across on a cargo-only voyage, departing on the 24th, but this had to be cancelled when the crew expected to man her failed to turn up. The strike action dragged on into September. Over 1,000 passengers, a near-capacity load, had been booked to sail on *Empress of Britain*'s 2nd September departure, but like the many passengers before them, they had to accept alternative ways of getting to their destinations.

The two 'Empresses' were berthed at the Gladstone Dock until the 10th September, when *Empress of England* was last able to resume her schedule. While she was docked at Montreal, at the end of that voyage, a series of fires broke out in five separate cabins. They caused heavy damage and were believed to have been started deliberately, probably by a still-disgruntled member of the crew. Despite this, the ship was able to sail as scheduled, but with the area of damaged cabins closed off. Of the liners that had been held up in Liverpool, *Empress of Britain* was the last to sail: she left for Canada on the 24th September on the midnight tide.

Since November, 1957, Canadian Pacific had been operating just three liners on the Liverpool to St. Lawrence run: the two new sisters and the thirty year-old *Empress of France*. With construction of the new flagship well advanced, *Empress of France* was to be retired. It was perhaps fitting that when she, the company's oldest liner, arrived in Liverpool on the 7th December, 1960 at the end of her 338th and final voyage, *Empress of England*, the company's newest ship, should also be there.

4
Empress of Canada

In January, 1959, the first keel plates of what would become the *Empress of Canada* were laid. Fourteen months later, on the 10th May, 1960, she was launched. On completion, she would be the largest passenger ship built on the Tyne since the *Mauretania* was constructed there over fifty years earlier. In February, 1961, when she was almost complete, *Empress of Canada* left the Vickers-Armstrongs Naval Yard for dry-docking at Swan, Hunter & Wigham Richardson's Wallsend facility. On the 3rd March, Vickers-Armstrongs gave their employees, and also employees of sub-contracting firms, the opportunity of showing their families around the new liner.

On the 7th March, 1961, ten months after her launching, the magnificent new Canadian Pacific Line flagship sailed from Wallsend to begin her trials voyage. After a series of runs on the Newbiggin measured mile, she set course at about midnight for the Clyde. On her way, she carried out a series of steaming trials, including those of her stabilisers and steering gear. She made her first appearance on the Clyde on Thursday, the 9th and anchored at the Tail of the Bank around mid-day. Early the following morning, she left for speed runs over the measured mile, returning to the Tail of the Bank that evening. Saturday saw her 'up anchor' early for circle and

Displaying her bulbous bow, *Empress of Canada* is seen moments before she is launched into the waters of the Tyne. She is proudly flying her builders' flag. *Laurence Dunn collection.*

A moment of tension and triumph: *Empress of Canada* **thunders down the ways, to meet her natural element for the first time.** *Laurence Dunn collection.*

other trials before she started two double runs off Arran on full power. Afterwards, she left the area for a 12-hour fuel and water consumption test prior to her arrival in the Mersey on Sunday evening.

Her performance during these trials was reported as being nothing short of splendid. On her full power run over the Arran mile, she had achieved a speed of 23 knots, which was over two knots greater than the designed service speed. Her master, Captain J. P. Dobson, Commodore of the Canadian Pacific fleet, said: "I am very pleased with what she has done. She is a beautiful ship and is a great credit to Tyneside."

She was returned to her builders for final adjustments and finishing touches and, once these were completed, she sailed on the 25th March for Liverpool, arriving there two days later. She would remain in Liverpool for almost a month and it was during this time that she was shown off to the shipping press and the travel trade.

Even with so many new and impressive liners all entering service during a relatively short time, the shipping press were nevertheless fulsome in their praise for the *Empress of Canada*. *The Shipping World* called her "this fine liner", while *Shipping and Transport* entitled an article about her 'Pride of the Tyne'. It went on to say that: "The

new vessel matches in speed, grace and luxurious passenger accommodation, everything that is best in British shipbuilding..... emphasises the ability of British yards to produce passenger tonnage that can compare for quality and finish with any competitors throughout the world." In a later article, which they devoted to her interiors, they stated: "*Empress of Canada* is a winner." The *Syren and Shipping* magazine said that she "continued the proud tradition of 'White Empresses'."

Empress of Canada was extremely graceful in appearance, with what was described as a clipper stem and with a cruiser stern, single funnel and streamlined foremast and stump mainmast. At 27,300 gross tons, she was at the time the largest vessel to call at Montreal: she had an overall length of 650 feet, a breadth of 86 feet 6 inches and a draught of 29 feet. Structurally, she differed from her earlier fleetmates mainly in the section between the navigation bridge and the funnel. Here, there was a covered games deck and there were also small sheltered observatory lounges to both port and starboard. She was built with an underwater hull similar to the two earlier ships but during model tests the problem of pitching had been given special attention, with the result that a bulbous bow was incorporated into the design. This, together with

Afloat at last, and surrounded by the débris of her launch, the new Canadian Pacific flagship is tended by ministering tugs. *Laurence Dunn collection.*

the Denny-Brown stabilisers, which could reduce a roll of 18 degrees to one of less than six degrees, would add considerably to the comfort of her passengers during bad weather. Special attention was also paid to the design of her rudder, which was planned for maximum manoeuvrability in the restricted waterways of the St. Lawrence.

The funnel, too, was of a slightly different design from that on the other two ships, but was still of a conventional shape with the company's red and white chequered house flag represented on either side. If there was any criticism to be made of the profile of *Empress of Canada*, it was with regard to the pair of cargo derricks that served Number 3 hatch. Being located so close to the bridge-front, they contributed to a rather heavy and untidy look, particularly when the ship was viewed from three-quarter bow.

The propelling machinery had been constructed by Vickers-Armstrongs (Engineers) Ltd. and incorporated the latest improvements in high-speed turbine and watertube boiler practice. It was nevertheless of the same basic design and output as that fitted into the two earlier ships and comprised of two sets of Vickers-Armstrongs Pametrada double-reduction geared turbines designed for a combined output of 27,000 s.h.p. in service and 30,000

s.h.p. maximum. It worked on the reheat system as developed by Fairfields, the builders of the *Empress of Britain*. Each main turbine unit consisted of an h.p. and i.p. turbine driving their own pinions at 4,195 r.p.m. and 3,425 r.p.m., respectively. They took steam at 600 il p.s.i., 850 deg. Fahr. and operated on the reheat cycle, whereby the h.p. exhaust was reheated to the initial temperature. Before it entered the i.p. turbine, the steam passed through two groups of nozzles and there was also an overload port, which by-passed the first three stages. One of the two groups of nozzles was controlled and the arrangement was such that steam was not available at the overload valve unless the nozzle control valve was open.

The main boiler installation consisted of two Foster Wheeler controlled superheat boilers and one Foster Wheeler reheat boiler. The arrangement of machinery was similar to that on the two previous ships: the propelling machinery slightly aft of amidships, with the boiler room forward, then the auxiliary machinery room, switchboard room, stabiliser compartment and refrigerating machinery space.

The construction of the new 'Empress' involved a combination of longitudinal and transverse framing, and employed welding to a far greater extent than was general

for a vessel of this class at that time. In addition, the sheerstrake and two strakes of plating about the waterline were of special welding quality steel and the scantlings of the frame and the shell forward were increased for ice stiffening. All butts were welded and there were only six riveted seams on each side, the frames in all cases being riveted. All the decks were welded. Special attention was given to the pillaring arrangement throughout the ship and, in view of the high stresses involved, an expansion joint was incorporated in the superstructure. The ship was sub-divided below the bulkhead deck by 11 watertight bulkheads; and above the bulkhead deck by six main fireproof divisions, giving seven main fireproof zones.

Notable in the external design were the large three-panelled windows along Empress Deck. These had been specially developed by the manufacturer, Beclawat and had a built-in handrail which enabled passengers to have unrestricted views whether they were seated or standing. This same treatment was extended to the large windows of the public rooms. Canadian Pacific had been somewhat in advance of many other shipowners in recognising the attraction and the advantages of fitting their ships with air-conditioning. Following the lead set by *Empress of Britain*, the first completely air-conditioned passenger vessel built in Britain, the '*Canada*' was fitted with the most modern system of air-conditioning, heating and ventilation.

Although she was fitted to carry her passengers in two classes: 192 in First Class and 856 in Tourist Class, no reference was made to either 'First' or 'Tourist' in the designation of the public rooms, thus enhancing the one-class status of the ship when cruising. Instead, all public rooms were given names, mainly Canadian. The main public rooms were located on, in descending order, Promenade, Empress, Upper, Main and Restaurant Decks, while the indoor Coral Pool was on Lower Deck. The two principal First Class rooms were forward on Promenade Deck and were called the Mayfair Room and the St. Lawrence Club. The First Class restaurant, Salle Frontenac, was on Restaurant Deck. Cabins and suites for those passengers travelling First Class were located forward on Empress Deck and amidships on Upper Deck.

The Tourist Class public rooms took the after part of Empress Deck: the Windsor Lounge and Banff Club. However, amidships and forward of the Windsor Lounge was the impressive, two-deck high Canada Room which, like the Empress Room on the two earlier ships, was available to both classes. A sizeable two-deck high cinema and an indoor pool were also open to passengers regardless of which class they were travelling in.

The décor of the public rooms aboard the *Empress of*

Canada was bright, vibrant and exciting, yet ignored any extremes or design gimmicks. Thus, her designers had created a ship of great style, richness, grace and individuality. Whereas aboard the previous two 'Empress' liners the interior styling had been distinctively British, on the *Empress of Canada* both the First and Tourist Class public rooms were decidedly North American in their blending of comfort, elegance and informality. The contrast between the two classes was slight, with the fact that they were located on separate decks further reducing any impression of different degrees of elegance. However, despite her bright, sunny and modern look, there were those who criticised the ship for being dull. The Banff Club was a particular target for criticism – not, in this case, because of dullness but because of its strongly Canadian Ranch-themed décor.

Nevertheless, the journal *Shipping* stated that the *Empress of Canada* was: "Undoubtedly a ship whose general décor, furnishings and accommodation are something which we have been waiting for in a big liner for some time." Responsibility for the interior design had been entrusted to two men: Mr. J. Patrick McBride, a partner in the firm of Glasgow architects McInnes, Gardner & Partners, and Mr. Paul Gell, a design consultant based in London. For the very creative Mr. Gell it was his first effort in ship design and shortly afterwards his work was also in evidence aboard the former *Saxonia* and *Ivernia* when they were transformed into *Carmania* and *Franconia*.

The Mayfair Room, the principal First Class lounge, had a colour scheme of deep rose contrasted with coffee and lilac. While this was charming during the daytime, its elegance was enhanced during the evening, when curtains were drawn across the broad curving windows on either side of the room to give a mural effect of spring trees in blossom against a background of ice blue. Following this decorative theme, a metal sculpture of a branch of blossom was set above the modern-styled fireplace on the sycamore panelled forward wall. Although this was essentially a square room, a circular effect was created by the gently curved windows and the curved front and aft bulkheads. This was enhanced by a shallow circular dome over the central part of the room. A section of carpet under this dome could be removed to reveal a dance floor.

Forward of Mayfair Room was the St. Lawrence Club, panelled in figured larch. Its principal colour scheme was blue and red. Two murals of the St. Lawrence River were used to decorate the room and four illustrations of famous ships were recessed into the panelling opposite the bar. Behind the bar were armorial plaques of French Canadian families associated with the river. The Study, which

Empress of Canada makes her way slowly down the Tyne en route for her trials. Onboard, workmen are still busily engaged giving her the 'finishing touches'. *Laurence Dunn collection.*

Looking every inch a classic liner, *Empress of Canada* moves smoothly through the water during her speed trials. *Laurence Dunn collection.*

functioned as a library and writing room, was panelled in laurelwood and leather and was the only First Class public room to be located on Empress Deck.

The Salle Frontenac, the First Class restaurant, was on two levels, the central area being sunken. The two levels were separated by jardinières and by a decorative balustrade in a silvery metal, with glass panels into which the Coat of Arms of the Count of Frontenac was worked in blue and gold. The colour scheme was of dark and light blue and featured a design of fleur-de-lys while panels of figured sycamore and Rio rosewood enhanced the walls. An interesting feature was that an arrangement of full-length drapes could 'shrink' the room when the First Class passenger complement was not enough to fill it.

For Tourist Class, the Windsor Lounge was the principal leisure space. It featured a dramatic and bold decorative scheme in shades of grey, blue, lemon and black. The panelling was in zebrano with laurelwood trim, except on the forward walls: these were covered in lemon leather and served as a background to several modern paintings by British artists. The Banff Club, which was the Tourist Class cocktail lounge, was at the after end of the enclosed accommodation and overlooked the wide open deck space of the Lido which, under cruising conditions, would be fitted with a portable swimming pool. The room was panelled by planks of Lebanon cedar. The serpentine bar, of solid teak, was fronted with cowhide panels, each of which had been tooled by authentic Canadian ranch brands. In the centre of the room was a birch dance floor, to either side of which were imaginatively styled carpets, the design of which was based upon native American tribal symbols and beadwork. The red, brown, yellow and blue shades in the carpets were carried though to the rest of the décor. The dance floor was flanked on either side by two pillars and by jardinières, all covered in yellow and brown mosaic tiles.

The Tourist Class Carleton Restaurant was a spacious room of bold design, in some contrast to the elegance of the Salle Frontenac. The dominating colours of coral and jade looked very attractive against the pale primavera and afromosia woods used in the panelling. Like the First Class restaurant, the Carleton was on two levels. Sweeping panoramic murals based on Canadian scenes were a major decorative feature of the room, which was pierced by the trunking for two engine room vents. These helped to break up the large mass of space into more intimate dining areas.

The Canada Room, on Empress Deck, was the largest public room on the ship. This ballroom, with a central quartic dome and gallery, was decorated in shades of gold, supposedly to represent the colours of ripening grain. In a lavish brochure issued by Canadian Pacific shortly before the ship entered service, the room was described as follows: "The Canadian theme, which influences the decoration of many of the public areas of *Empress of Canada*, is well expressed on Empress Deck – notably in the Canada Room. Here lavish fenestration, brightly coloured walls and curtaining combine with generous architectural proportions to recreate indoors the bright, sunny outdoor feeling of Canada's wide open spaces. Canadian maple and birch in the parquetry dance floor,

relieved by mahogany, are surrounded by a specially designed and woven carpet, patterned with formalised designs of the symbolic wild flowers of the ten Provinces of Canada. Glazed screens, decorated with wheel-cut Canadian flora, flank the wide bow windows opening to the covered promenade outside. Walls panelled in figured willow gain contrast from bubinga and mahogany treatments, and a metal balustrade separates the raised area at the ends and sides from the dance floor. Two decks high, the Canada Room has an interesting sitting-out gallery overlooking the dance floor, reached by currently characteristic open-tread stairs moulded to the curve of the orchestra back screen. At the forward end of the room, a modern sculptured panel in wood and metal overlay epitomises natural elements of Canada. More than twenty feet above the dance floor, concealed lighting in the shallow dome can be controlled to the mood of the music. For the enjoyment of Tourist and First Class passengers, the Canada Room is accessible from the Windsor Lounge through wide glass doors that open an eighty-yard vista to

Stern views and admiring glances from the passengers of a Mersey ferry as the new flagship departs Liverpool on her maiden voyage on the 24th April, 1961. *Laurence Dunn collection.*

the deck abaft the Banff Club, and from the shopping centre forward. Coffee tables with tops of mosaic and hardwood are interspersed with tub and lounge chairs, upholstered in fabrics and leathers that pick up the bright notes of the carpet, which has an excellent foil in the plain rich green of the curtains. New in thought and distinctive in design and colouring, this magnificent room is reminiscent of earlier steamships of the Canadian Pacific fleet, famous 'Empresses' whose spacious and gracious saloons echoed waltz strains and the laughter and gay conversation of more leisured generations.''

Throughout the public rooms were found works of original art, carved wood and etched glass panels, oil paintings, prints, sculpture and murals ranging through factual to fanciful. The furniture was contemporary in style, clean of line, well-proportioned and comfortable.

For children travelling Tourist Class, there was The Den, a wide and spacious room located at the after end of the Promenade Deck. It had wide folding and hinged screens leading out onto the open deck. During cruises, The Den could be converted into a verandah café and bar. The Cinema, sited on Main Deck forward of the First Class entrance hall and staircase, was provided with separate dual access from both classes of accommodation. It rose through two decks; and an average clear height of 15 feet was attained over a raked floor so arranged that there was uninterrupted vision from all seating points. There were seats for 210, those at the after end being allocated to First Class passengers. The screen was adjustable to take wide-screen and 'Vista Vision' projections. The Cinema was also to be used for religious services and a built-in enclosed altar cabinet was incorporated into the design. As already mentioned, the indoor pool was down on the Lower Deck. Its name, Coral Pool, was deliberately chosen as a play on the initial letters of the company title.

Both the enclosed and the open promenade decks were relatively narrow. However, the enclosed promenades featured quite high overheads. Very unusually, the bulkheads of these promenades had bright splashes of colour, which reflected the scheme of the room to be found beyond the bulkhead. The outboard bulkhead of the Mayfair Room was painted a soft rose pink, while that of the Windsor Lounge was royal blue. A pleasant area where passengers could lounge in deck chairs was the First Class enclosed deck, just forward of the St. Lawrence Club: full-length windows gave a view out over the bow. First Class passengers also had two other splendid observation points, conservatory-like spaces on either side of the Games Room, located high up on Sun Deck.

As was to be expected, all the cabins in First Class were provided with a private toilet and either a bath or a shower. The walls were veneered and had glass fibre acoustic ceilings. To give colour contrast, certain spaces had textured insets to the panelling in the way of bed recesses. Built-in furniture was matching, while other loose pieces were in a darker solid hardwood. Different colour schemes were used. For instance, Cabin 26, forward on Empress Deck, had walls panelled in blister-figured Canadian maple with the loose furniture in French walnut. A specially-designed Wilton carpet in tones of brown and gold covered the floor, while the upholstery to the chairs was in yellow tweed and the curtain drapes were in striped orange, lilac and white. The sanitary ware in the bathroom was pale yellow.

A single berth cabin, number 4 on Upper Deck, had its walls panelled in grey dyed, figured sycamore with fitments of the same wood. The carpet was indigo and gold and chair coverings were in orange tweed. The curtains were orange, blue and green. This cabin could be linked with the adjoining two-berth cabin by an enclosed vestibule, thereby forming a suite. In Cabin 16 on Upper Deck, the walls and fitments were of light figured willow, with other furniture in rosewood. The carpet was grey and rose and the curtains were rose and white. One of the five-roomed Studio Suites, number 51, also on Upper Deck, featured a patterned floral carpet in tones of green and vermilion throughout. Yellow and green fabrics were used in the bedrooms and the wall veneer was figured aspen.

The Tourist Class cabins were located aft on Upper Deck (there was also a block of eighteen just forward of these which were interchangeable between classes as the need dictated), on Main Deck and aft on Restaurant Deck. All of them were of the one bed plus one upper berth type or had two beds and two folding upper berths; more than half of them were of the latter type. Nearly seventy per cent were provided with private toilet facilities and a number of them also had private showers. There were six different decorative schemes. The floors were covered in marbled linoleum with a rug, rather than with fitted carpets, and bed covers and curtains picked up one of the colours in the rugs.

Travel writer Denny Bond Beattie, Jnr. wrote: "While there is little difference between the public rooms of both classes, there is a substantial difference when it comes to the cabins. First Class staterooms are large and lush. Drawer and closet space is excellent, with good space for luggage. Tourist cabins are rather Spartan. Nevertheless, they are attractive and comfortable. Bulkheads are light-toned; spreads and drapes are a smart modern print on a neutral background. The furniture consists of a combination dresser-dressing table-desk of light wood and plastic; and a bench or straight-backed chair. Lighting is excellent and the bathrooms are compact in size. I would say that these Tourist cabins are comparable to those on the *Atlantic* but not up to those on the *Gripsholm*."

As well as having accommodation for just over 1,000 passengers, *Empress of Canada* was able to carry a considerable quantity of cargo: 262,000 cubic feet of it was general cargo, while 16,170 cubic feet was refrigerated. There was also the facility for her to carry 344 tons of cargo oil. Her holds were arranged two forward and two aft and access to them all was by means of five trunked hatchways. The weather deck hatches, Numbers 1 and 2, were fitted with steel covers and Numbers 3 and 4 (port and starboard) and Number 5 were of the flush type. MacGregor hatch covers were fitted at various points within the hatch trunks themselves, those in Number 2 hatch being of sufficient strength to take motor cars at all levels. For bulk-carrying purposes, Numbers 2 and 5 lower holds were fitted with grain dividers.

Empress of Canada had a crew of 510. Her officers were accommodated forward on Sports Deck, just below the bridge. The crew recreation room was located forward on Upper Deck, along with accommodation for 27 crewmembers. Further crew accommodation was forward on Restaurant Deck and through most of Lower Deck. The crew mess was also on this deck.

The commander of the new flagship, Captain J. P. Dobson, was an ex-'Conway Boy', who had joined the company after serving as a midshipman on the *Gloucestershire*, a Bibby Line ship acting as an auxiliary cruiser on convoy duties with the 10th Cruiser Squadron in the 1914-18 War. He had served in various Canadian Pacific ships and obtained his master's and extra master's certificates in 1926. In 1939, he had been the navigating officer aboard the *Empress of Australia* when she took King George VI and Queen Elizabeth to Canada. During the Second World War, he had commanded a group of minesweepers and, for his services, was promoted commander R.N.R. and awarded the D.S.C. (Distinguished Service Cross). After the War, he rejoined Canadian Pacific and took his first command, the new 10,000-ton cargo liner *Beaverglen*. Later, he commanded the *Beavercove, Empress of Australia*, the previous *Empress of Canada, Empress of France, Empress of Scotland* and *Empress of Britain*.

Commenting on his new vessel, Captain Dobson said that much thought had gone into the design of the navigating bridge, especially into the fitting-out of the wheelhouse. Naval architects had sought the advice of the company's captains and navigating officers and the result was the concensus of all that could be achieved within the limitations of the complete ship's design. Immediately one entered the wheelhouse, the eye was caught by the long chart table on the starboard side, with its mass of navigational equipment. A number of ships had already at that time been fitted with similar special tables, the object being to reduce the necessity of having to go into the chart room to consult charts and instruments – thereby helping to prevent the accidents that could happen when the watch-keeper's attention was unavoidably diverted. In the *Empress of Canada*'s wheelhouse, the layout of the chart table received special attention. It was placed to starboard of the helmsman and was in such a position that an officer standing at the table could see the gyro steering compass and also the repeater compass above the wheelhouse windows. He could also look over the top of the instrument panel and sight the horizon.

The Canadian Pacific deep sea fleet now consisted of the cargo vessels *Beavercove, Beaverdell, Beaverford, Beaverglen* and *Beaverlake*, all of which had been built

Two decks high, the modernistic Canada Room was open to both First and Tourist Class passengers.
Laurence Dunn collection.

between 1944 and 1947; and the three passenger liners *Empress of Britain*, *Empress of England* and *Empress of Canada*.

At the time of *Empress of Canada*'s entry into service, the World was enjoying a renaissance of ocean liner construction despite the fact that many thousands of trans-oceanic travellers were beginning to turn more and more to air travel. Splendid new liners were being built for most of the major routes around the World. Cunard were poised to place an order for a new Atlantic liner, code-named 'Q3', to replace the *Queen Mary*. The editorial in the 10th May, 1961 issue of *The Syren & Shipping* wrote: "It is difficult to understand the extravagant criticisms in Parliament last week and in the national Press on the proposed subsidy for the *Queen Mary* replacement ship. The nasty remark was made in the House of Commons that while the Russians were launching a man into space, we were launching a white elephant into the ocean. No one said this about the recently completed *Oriana*, *Canberra* or *Empress of Canada*…"

These few lines of that editorial really set the tone of the day, for despite the considerable increases in the number of passengers travelling by air, there was still great enthusiasm and optimism for the shipbuilding industry and for the future of travel by sea. Indeed, many of the very long-haul liner routes were continuing to flourish. The shipyards of Britain were playing a very central rôle in this ocean liner renaissance. In the period between April, 1960 and October, 1963, fourteen major liners were completed, nine of them in British yards. All of these ships were designed and built principally with point-to-point voyages in mind. With just one exception, they divided their passengers by class; and the design of only four of them acknowledged a possible cruising rôle – and even that was secondary. In June, 1960, the *Windsor Castle* was completed as flagship of the Union-Castle Line; in April and September, Royal Mail Lines took delivery of *Aragon* and *Arlanza*; and the year ended with the strikingly designed *Oriana* being delivered to Orient Line. 1961 was a vintage year: on the 17th January, a further Union-Castle liner, *Transvaal Castle* was launched. In March, *Empress of Canada* departed on her trials voyage and in May, the new P&O flagship *Canberra* departed on hers. Also undertaking her trials at exactly the same time was the *Principe Perfeito*, which had been built by Swan, Hunter & Wigham Richardson for Portuguese owners. Shaw, Savill's *Northern Star* was launched on the 27th June.

Sadly, the combined effects of competition from the jet aircraft and the ever-increasing price of fuel, as well as labour costs and, to some extent, the containerisation of the cargo trade, would ensure that the majority of this last great flowering of 'ships of state' would spend most of their careers as full-time cruise ships. Just one of those fourteen liners managed to serve for seventeen years on the service for which she was designed. The rest spent far less time in the rôles for which they had been envisaged. In fact, just four months after the introduction of *Empress of Canada* into the St. Lawrence service, Canadian Pacific Airlines obtained a licence from the Air Transport Board of Canada to fly to London. In the event, CPA was unable to obtain landing rights from the British government and ultimately the licence was withdrawn in 1965.

Thus, it was against this somewhat confused backdrop of confidence in ocean liner development, yet increasing growth in transoceanic air travel (particularly across the Atlantic) that, on the 24th April, 1961, *Empress of Canada* prepared to depart Liverpool on her maiden voyage. During her twenty-seven day stay in the Mersey, she had twice encountered her fleet mate *Empress of Britain*, which by that time was back on the Canadian service. Then, just three days before the new flagship set sail on her maiden voyage, she was joined in port by *Empress of England*, which had arrived from New York on completion of her series of winter cruises. As *Empress of Canada* left the Mersey with 900 passengers aboard, she was within range of the Ulster Television signal. Sets had been especially installed in her lounges to receive the Ulster Television transmission *An Empress Sails*. As with *Empress of England*, a documentary had been made about the ship, from her keel-laying to completion.

The new liner made her first arrival in Canada when she reached Quebec on the 1st May. Her passengers had undoubtedly looked forward to the 1,000 miles of the sheltered waters of the St. Lawrence after encountering 30-foot head-on waves during a 60 m.p.h. gale while crossing the Atlantic. By all accounts, the ship rode the storm magnificently. She was scheduled to make ten round trips to the St. Lawrence that season, the final one ending in Liverpool on the 17th November.

Shortly after *Empress of Canada* entered service, Canadian Pacific announced the expansion of their already diverse empire by the introduction of a credit card. It was claimed to be the first to be issued by a transport company including both air and sea travel. It was valid for passenger travel on Canadian Pacific's international and domestic air routes and for air express and air cargo charges within Canada. It also covered travel on the company's 'Empress' liners in both trans-Atlantic and cruise service. In addition, it was honoured by all Canadian Pacific hotels across Canada and was accepted for telegraphs, cablegrams and radiograms at Canadian Pacific telegraph offices in Canada and at Western Union offices in the United States. It was also valid for Hertz car rentals. The aim was to provide customers with convenient credit facilities for travel to five continents. For air and sea transport, it was accepted by appointed travel agencies and at all Canadian Pacific offices and general agencies anywhere in the World.

With a fleet of three modern and virtually new ships, Canadian Pacific were ideally positioned to offer an extensive cruise programme during the winter months. The entry into service of the *Empress of Canada* enabled them, during the winter of 1961-62, to proffer a series of cruises almost comparable to those undertaken by the pre-War *Empress of Britain* in the 'thirties. Being the flagship, the new liner took over the rôle of operating the prestige cruise programme out of New York. Three Caribbean cruises were planned: the first, over Christmas and the New Year, being 14 days long, while the other two were both 15-day trips. These were then to be followed by a lengthy Mediterranean cruise.

However, it seemed that this first series of cruises was destined to get off to a disappointing start. Having spent nearly a month in Liverpool being overhauled and made ready, *Empress of Canada* was being gently manoeuvred from her berth to the passenger terminal in the shadow of the impressive Liver Building when she struck the dock wall. No damage was done other than to her dignity, but

Seen here before the central chandelier was installed, the First Class lounge, the Mayfair Room, was a successful combination of the modern and the formal. *Laurence Dunn collection.*

large black streaks marred her once-pristine hull. She was under the command of Captain C. L. de H. Bell and he was far from pleased, demanding that the defaced areas be repainted before the passengers arrived. The *Empress of Canada* was the flagship and she should look like the flagship! With her freshly painted white hull once again gleaming despite the grey and cold winter day, she sailed for New York at 5.30 pm on the 12th December: in fact her departures from Liverpool were always set for that time.

The Canadian Pacific publicity and marketing departments had been hard at work planning the arrival of the new 'Empress' in New York. As she made her way up the Hudson River towards the pier normally used by the Furness Withy Line ships, she would be accorded the usual maiden voyage welcome, with fanfares, bunting and streamers as well as plumes of spray from escorting fireboats. Having left England on a cold and wintry day, she arrived in even more unpleasant conditions on the 19th December, steaming slowly into New York harbour and up towards her Manhattan berth. The elaborate pomp and circumstance of her welcome had been cancelled: the city was shrouded in freezing fog.

On that first Caribbean cruise, she was in St. Thomas on Christmas Eve and Christmas Day, whilst 1962 was welcomed in as she steamed towards Port au Prince. The other two cruises were, of course, a welcome escape from the winter chill of New York and, with her good speed, *Empress of Canada* made short work of the voyage down the east coast of America, taking just three days to reach the balmy warmth of St. Thomas.

Canadian Pacific went to great lengths to promote the Mediterranean and Greek Isles cruise. Of sixty days and with calls at thirty ports, it was of epic proportions and equalled those undertaken by some of the legendary liners of the 'twenties and 'thirties. It was, of course, also similar to some of the cruises operated by Cunard's *Caronia*. Therefore, it was hardly surprising that Canadian Pacific advertised it extensively. "Announcing the new *Empress of Canada*'s fabulous Mediterranean – Greek Isles Cruise. Never before a Mediterranean cruise so all-encompassing! Plan now to be along on the most exciting Mediterranean cruise ever! Two full months of exploration of the world's most fascinating sea, at its best in sunny Spring!... a never-to-be-forgotten panorama of the Mediterranean, the sights, sounds, colours of 60 centuries of history from the

Canadian Pacific's Lisbon agents celebrate the launch of the 'novo paquete' *Empress of Canada*.
Luís Miguel Correia collection.

Stone Age to World War II... every one of the 14,240 miles is timed to give you the most daylight hours ashore. Shore visits up to four days; excursions if you wish to Cairo, Jerusalem, Rome, Madrid, Monte Carlo. Fares from $1,675. This may be the most sought-after cruise of all times..."

Empress of Canada departed New York on this remarkable odyssey on the 9th February, 1962, calling first at Tenerife and then at Madeira. It was there, in the bay of Funchal harbour, that she encountered *Empress of England*, which was operating a seventeen-day cruise from Liverpool to the Atlantic islands and North Africa. *Empress of Canada* then made calls in Morocco, Tunisia and Malta before arriving in Alexandria. From there, she went on to Israel and Lebanon before calling at several Greek islands en route for one of the highlights of the cruise, Istanbul. Onward she went, to Athens and then up the Adriatic to Venice; around Italy to Sicily and Naples; then Villefranche for the delights of the French Riviera. Calls were made at Barcelona, Majorca, Malaga and Oran before the 'Canada' bade farewell to the Mediterranean. Lisbon was her final port before she headed back to New York, her passengers doubtless burdened with souvenirs and with their senses spinning from such a rich mix of so many different cultures. In two months they had called at more ports than many ships visit when on cruises around the World.

Empress of Canada arrived back in New York on the 11th April, 1962 and the following day she sailed for Liverpool. Despite being the glamorous new flagship of the Canadian Pacific fleet, she was carrying just 66 First Class passengers and a reduced compliment in Tourist Class. New York was not a regular terminal for the 'Empresses' on the Atlantic service and as a result they did not attract many passengers for the return to the United Kingdom after their cruising seasons. Also, while *Empress of Canada* had been making her mark as a cruise ship, the sensational new French Line flagship, *France*, had entered service on the prestige route between New York and the Channel ports.

While *Empress of Canada* had been cruising from New York, both *Empress of England* and *Empress of Britain* were introduced to the British cruising public. *Empress of England* had completed her 1961 series of sailings to the St. Lawrence with her arrival back at Liverpool on the 13th December. She remained there for a month, departing on her very first British-based cruise on the 13th January, 1962. It was a fourteen-day trip on the popular route down to Madeira, the Canary Islands, Casablanca, Tangier and Lisbon. Then, on the 30th January she sailed for New York via Greenock and St. John. From New York she departed on a fourteen-day Caribbean cruise. Whilst this was followed by a further fourteen-day trip, the remaining two cruises were somewhat different from those she had made out of New York in previous years. One was of just ten days, to Nassau and St. Thomas, and the other was of a mere eight days and included her first ever call at Bermuda as well as a stop at Nassau. For this latter cruise, departing New York on the 26th March, she had been chartered by the College of General Practice of Canada, probably making this the first medical convention held at sea. On the 4th April, she left New York for Liverpool to resume her St. Lawrence sailings.

Earlier, on the 17th December, *Empress of England* had made news in a rather dramatic way while quietly berthed in Liverpool's Gladstone Dock, waiting for the weather to moderate before she entered drydock for her annual winter overhaul. Her aft lines gave way as violent storm-force winds increased, causing her to swing round on her forward ropes. Although her stern anchor was dropped, it did not prevent her from striking a concrete projection, causing damage along twenty feet of her side, and then coming to rest with her stern hard against the cargo liner *Hindustan*. As a result, the dock was blocked for about twenty hours.

For *Empress of Britain*, the year 1961 had not been the best of times. Her 18th April trans-Atlantic sailing had been delayed by 24 hours due to a strike by members of the unofficial National Seamen's Reform Movement. The action was called in protest at the dismissal of three crew from the engine room but, after negotiations in which Canadian Pacific agreed to re-instate them, the ship was eventually able to sail. In order to maintain her schedule, passengers were embarked while she was still in the Gladstone Dock and the 200 other passengers who should have joined her at Greenock were taken to Liverpool by train and boarded her in mid-river. The following month, mechanical problems were the cause of another delayed sailing. The ship had been due to depart Montreal on the 19th May with 780 passengers aboard when her port main gear-wheel was discovered to have teeth damaged.

Temporary repairs were made, enabling her to sail at 8am the following morning.

Her 14th November departure was also disrupted by labour difficulties. In this instance, some of the deck and catering crew walked off just before the ship was due to sail. They were demanding the dismissal of a boatswain. It was not until the 16th, almost 36 hours behind schedule and with crew members brought from elsewhere in the country, that *Empress of Britain* was able to sail. On this occasion, there were just 350 passengers aboard. To make up some of the lost time, it was decided that she would not call at Greenock: instead, the 80 passengers who had been expected to board there were picked up by the rival *Carinthia*.

Empress of Britain maintained her wintertime trans-Atlantic programme through until the 13th January, 1962. It was not known at the time, of course, but this would turn out to be the last time a Canadian Pacific liner would offer such sailings during the winter months. The '*Britain*' was out of service for a month being overhauled. She then sailed, on the 13th February, on the second Canadian Pacific cruise to be operated from Britain that winter. She followed a very similar route to that of her sister, except that she ventured as far south as St. Vincent in the Cape Verde Islands. It was a clear indication of things to come. However, by early March she was back on the Atlantic, with just one sailing to St. John before resuming her St. Lawrence service by the end of the month. One of her trans-Atlantic sailings broke the usual Liverpool – St. Lawrence pattern: on the 1st December, 1962, she departed Montreal for Southampton, where she arrived on the 7th. It was the first time she had been there since her pre-maiden voyage shake-down cruise over six years earlier. The following day, she continued across the North Sea to Bremerhaven. Her final westbound crossing for that year departed the German port on the 10th December and was direct to St. John (NB). She was back in Liverpool again by the 28th December.

In all, the three 'Empresses' had made thirty-three round-trip sailings between the United Kingdom and the St. Lawrence ports of Quebec and Montreal between the 27th March and the 7th December, 1962. Never again would the impressive White Empress fleet offer such an extensive programme of Atlantic sailings.

Visiting Lisbon towards the end of her 61-day Mediterranean cruise in 1962, *Empress of Canada* shows off her elegant lines as she makes her way along the Tagus. *Luis Miguel Correia collection.*

A night-time view of *Empress of Canada*'s sculptural funnel, made even more striking by floodlighting. *Laurence Dunn collection.*

5
Changes

On the 22nd November, 1962, *Empress of Canada* ended her St. Lawrence sailings for the year. She was overhauled and made ready for an extensive series of cruises that would run through until late the following April. On the 21st December, she sailed from Liverpool on her first cruise from that port. It was almost a repeat of the itinerary of the one *Empress of Britain* had operated from Liverpool the previous February, going as far south as the Cape Verde Islands. It ended, however, at Southampton, with the *Empress of Canada* making her maiden arrival in the Hampshire port on the 7th January, 1963. (This was the second call by a Canadian Pacific liner in a month.) From there she set off on a twenty eight-day trip to the West Indies, the kind of cruise that made the 'Empress' ships, and more specifically *Empress of Canada*, very special. She has been described as a ship with a very distinctive air about her: something that set her apart from her fleetmates and from other ships, an indefinable quality that seemed to say: "This is the flagship of the Canadian Pacific Line." However, there were those, more familiar with the *Empress of England*, who described her atmosphere as "chilly and too posh".

Nevertheless, her West Indies cruise was a glamorous escape from Britain's winter and one that seemed well-suited to the luxurious flagship. She departed Southampton at 2pm on Thursday, the 10th January and late that evening she made a brief call at Le Havre to embark continental passengers, departing at midnight. Her first call was at Las Palmas, a ten-hour stay on the 14th January. Then it was a five-day Atlantic crossing to Port of Spain, Trinidad. At 8am on the 23rd, *Empress of Canada* arrived in Kingston, Jamaica and she remained there until 1pm the following day. She then threaded her way through the islands of the Bahamas and arrived at Port Everglades on the 26th for a nineteen-hour stay. After six more leisurely days at sea, she was berthed at Funchal for eighteen hours. Homeward, the grand flagship made a brief early morning call at Le Havre before arriving back in Southampton at the more civilised hour of 3pm.It had been a wintertime cruise in the British manner: of its 28 days, over 19 had been spent at sea.

Empress of Canada remained in Southampton for four days, departing on the 12th February on a leisurely 7-day crossing to New York. This was followed by a virtual repeat of the lengthy Mediterranean cruise she had made the previous spring: only on this occasion she called at 24 ports during the 60 days. Her passengers were given ample opportunities to explore, with lengthy stops in most ports. In many cases she stayed overnight, while in Beirut, Haifa, Venice and Naples she made a two-night call and, so that her passengers could undertake long excursions to see the splendours of ancient Egypt, she lay in Alexandria for 3 nights. Unfortunately, she would never undertake such an extensive or exotic cruise again.

On the 25th April, she departed New York for Liverpool to resume her regular service to the St. Lawrence. During her first two years in service, *Empress of Canada* had operated flawlessly. However, she arrived late at Quebec on the 18th September, 1963, due to a combination of bad weather and slight engine trouble. There were 600 passengers aboard for the return voyage, of whom 172 were scheduled to disembark at Greenock. However, engine troubles also affected that return voyage and the call Greenock had to be cancelled to allow extra time for repairs to me made. She arrived back in Liverpool on the 27th September, 30 hours late, only for one of her propellers to be fouled when she was being manoeuvred by a tug. The repairs were effected during the weekend of the 28th and 29th and *Empress of Canada* was able to sail on schedule on the 1st October.

That voyage, too, proved to be an eventful one. A strike by longshoremen was causing considerable disruption to shipping traffic in the St. Lawrence. *Empress of Canada*, with 409 passengers aboard, arrived off strike-bound Quebec on the 8th October. She made a second attempt to dock the following day but was still unable to do so: again, she returned to her mid-river anchorage. Meanwhile, Cunard Line's *Carinthia*, alerted to the problems, was diverted to Halifax to disembark her 203 passengers. As it seemed unlikely that *Empress of Canada* would be allowed to dock, she left on the 10th and also headed for Halifax. There, she disembarked her passengers, unloaded her cargo and embarked her east-bound passengers, who had to be transferred from Quebec to Halifax by rail. Fortunately, the problems on the St. Lawrence had been solved before, on her next round voyage, she made her final calls of the season at Quebec and Montreal.

Back in Liverpool on the 7th November, she was given her usual overhaul before departing for St. John and New York on the 7th December. Her winter 1963/64 season of cruises from New York was to be far less exciting or far-reaching than those of her previous two winters: seven trips to the Caribbean. These were undoubtedly of broader appeal, and therefore far easier to sell, than 60-day Mediterranean cruises. In fact, it would be *Empress of Canada*'s older sisters that would be making even more of an impact as long-haul cruise ships over the following months.

From January to April, 1963, both *Empress of Britain* and *Empress of England* were employed on cruises. The *Empress of Britain* undertook a series of four to Madeira, the Canary Islands, Morocco and Lisbon. Meanwhile, *Empress of England* was positioned in New York, also operating a programme of four cruises, but in her case down to the Caribbean. One was a nineteen-day itinerary, two were of fourteen days and one was of sixteen days. By April, all three ships were together again on the St. Lawrence run: it would be their final summer together in the trade for which they were built. Between them, they made twenty-eight round-trip sailings.

Empress of Britain's 30th April voyage from Liverpool

proved to be a newsworthy one. While in mid-Atlantic, an elderly lady passenger became ill and required treatment that necessitated frequent transfusions of a very particular type of blood. When it became clear that further supplies of plasma were urgently required, a signal was sent to the coast guard stationed in Argentia, Newfoundland. Having established the liner's position, course and speed, a Royal Canadian Air Force rescue plane dropped the vital plasma in the early morning of the 5th May. The package was picked up by one of the ship's boats. Two days later, *Empress of Britain* arrived in Quebec.

The introduction of the passenger-carrying jet aircraft in the late 1950s had an immediate effect on the number of passengers crossing the North Atlantic by sea. From a high of over one million in 1957/58, it fell to around 800,000 and remained steady at that point for a while. Although there was another sudden drop to the 700,000 mark in 1961, by 1962 there was a slight increase back to the 800,000 level: inspired presumably by the introduction of the new French Line flagship *France*. Nevertheless, the decline had really begun and 1963 marked the start of a rapid fall. Even though the airlines were taking more and more of the trans-Atlantic passenger trade, they were not financially very successful. Quite curiously, several shipowners actually purchased interests in airlines, possibly the most interesting example being the formation by Cunard Line and B.O.A.C. of a joint operating company to run airliners on certain routes. Canadian Pacific, of course, had been involved in airline operations for many years.

The Canadian trade was suffering badly enough for Home Lines to withdraw the *Homeric* from the service in late 1963 and transfer her to full-time cruising duties. At the time, they had the 39,421-gross tons *Oceanic* under construction, designed specifically for the Northern Europe to Canada service. The decision was taken to complete her as a cruise ship, a move which, despite all the indications, was regarded as sheer folly. In fact, she became one of the most successful cruise ships of her day.

Meanwhile, the shipping press was lamenting the fact that so many Britons were completely inexperienced in sea travel. In an editorial in the 13th June, 1963 issue of *Shipbuilding and Shipping Record*, the comment was made: "To the middle-aged generation of today, the sea conjures up wartime voyages in comfort-lacking troopships. Perhaps continuous publicity by the purveyors of sea travel will ultimately bring the average British citizen to a realisation of what the sea should mean to us all. One organisation which is doing invaluable work in this direction is Ocean Travel Development. For seven years past, in conjunction with passenger liner companies and with travel agents, O.T.D. has organised an Ocean Travel Fortnight. Last year, over 8,000 people went aboard passenger ships at British ports and for this year's Fortnight (November 2-16) more ships will be made available for this purpose. There will be 'open ships' at London Tilbury, Southampton, Liverpool, Newcastle and Glasgow."

Another organisation which was doing its best, in a rather novel way, to lure people to take cruising holidays was the Travel Savings Association. The TSA, as it was more commonly known, was headed by a South African entrepreneur, Max Wilson, and promoted cheap 'no frills' cruises. The potential passengers paid instalments into TSA's special savings scheme, eventually using the money to buy inexpensive cruises or other holidays. Initially, the scheme seemed to meet with great success. The Pacific Steam Navigation Company's *Reina del Mar* had already been chartered and then TSA announced the charter of the recently retired P&O liner *Stratheden* from December, 1963 to January, 1964. Canadian Pacific, too, were more than happy to accept a charter from TSA for both *Empress of Britain* and *Empress of England*, beginning in the latter part of 1963. In fact, they were sufficiently enthusiastic about the Travel Savings concept to acquire a 51% controlling interest in the new company. Union-Castle and Royal Mail Lines also bought stakes in it.

Empress of Britain had sailed from Liverpool on the 24th September, 1963 on what would turn out to be her final voyage to the St. Lawrence. On this occasion, she called at just Greenock outbound and at Quebec, arriving there on the 1st October and departing on the 3rd. She was back in Liverpool on the 10th, at the end of her 108th round voyage to Canada. On the 25th October, with over 900 passengers aboard, she sailed from Liverpool on her first cruise for TSA, calling at Corunna, Tangier, Villefranche, Valencia and Gibraltar in fourteen days. The next cruise was thirteen days long but called only at Palma and Lisbon.

However, Mr. Wilson and the TSA had more ambitious plans for both 'Empresses', plans that would take full advantage of Canadian Pacific's forward-thinking designs for the ships, which made them fully suited to tropical cruising. *Empress of England* had arrived in Liverpool on the 14th November at the end of her last Atlantic crossing of the season. After disembarking her passengers and spending several days discharging cargo, she was given a brief overhaul to make her ready for TSA's programme. On the 28th November, she embarked on what would be the most exciting programme of her career. She was bound for Cape Town: from there she would undertake a series of cruises that would not only take her across the South Atlantic to Brazil and Argentina but also up the east coast of South Africa and to exotic ports in the Indian Ocean. Her journey down to South Africa was more in the nature of a liner voyage as she made just one call, at Dakar on the 4th/5th December, and arrived in Cape Town on the 13th. On the 16th, she was given a splendid send-off, with crowds at the dockside and multi-coloured streamers being thrown from the ship, as she departed on a 24-day cruise to Santos and Rio de Janeiro over Christmas and New Year.

On the 4th December, after a twelve-day refit, *Empress of Britain* followed in her sister's wake, heading for South Africa. Amongst her passengers she had some 570 emigrants who were travelling under the South African government's assisted passage scheme. A call was made at Dakar on the 10th/11th December and the ship arrived at Cape Town on the 19th. She was scheduled to operate two cruises across the South Atlantic. So, after a two-day stay in Cape Town, she once again followed her sister, but on a more extensive itinerary. She arrived in Buenos Aires (where she berthed overnight on the 30th and 31st), and continued on to Montevideo, Santos and Rio de Janeiro. On the 17th January, 1964, she repeated this cruise. *Empress of England* also sailed on the same itinerary between the 11th January and the 4th February. However, changes were being made to the operations of TSA, which

THE TRAVEL SAVINGS ASSOCIATION PRESENTS

EMPRESS OF BRITAIN

A brochure of the short-lived Travel Savings Association, who chartered *Empress of Britain* for a series of cruises from South Africa. *Chris Mason collection*

affected both 'Empresses' and resulted in a totally revised schedule for *Empress of Britain*. The remaining cruises that she had been scheduled to operate out of South Africa were instead to be undertaken by the *Reina del Mar*. *Empress of Britain* was now to return to Europe to operate a programme of cruises there.

TSA's original charter of *Empress of Britain* had been for five years. However, when companies other than Canadian Pacific acquired an interest, a cancellation clause was added, allowing TSA the option to terminate the charter at certain stages. Early in 1964, they exercised this option, seeking withdrawal as from the 5th January, 1965. Thus, it seemed that *Empress of Britain*'s departure date of the 13th from Cape Town was singularly appropriate. Shortly afterwards, it was announced that the savings scheme would in any event be abandoned at the end of the year. Despite having been launched in a blaze of publicity, the Travel Savings Association had not developed into the success that had been envisaged.

The two sisters were in Cape Town together on the 10th February, 1964 and *Empress of Britain* sailed on the 13th for Liverpool, again calling en route at Dakar. Meanwhile, *Empress of England* had already steamed off in the opposite direction. She called at Port Elizabeth, East London, Durban, Lourenço Marques, Mauritius and Mombasa, returning to Cape Town via the South African ports. On the 8th March, she sailed again on the Argentinian and Brazilian itinerary from Cape Town and then, on the 3rd April, she too sailed northwards from Cape Town, heading for Liverpool. The remains of the TSA operation, together with the charter of the *Reina del Mar*, were to be taken over by Union-Castle.

With the decline in the numbers of passengers crossing the Atlantic by sea, Canadian Pacific had come to the inevitable conclusion that they could no longer justify operating three liners on the St. Lawrence service. The

eight year-old *Empress of Britain* was made available for sale. In 1955, 55,000 passengers had arrived in Canada from Europe by sea, while 47,000 had come by air. By 1960, while there had been a very slight increase to 56,000 arriving by sea, the number travelling by air had risen enormously to 149,000. With remarkable understatement, Canadian Pacific said: "The economics of passenger operations are not what they should be." Sadly, from northern Europe they were not, but trans-Atlantic liner services from Mediterranean ports were flourishing. By the time *Empress of Britain* had arrived back in Liverpool on the 28th February, 1964, Canadian Pacific had sold her to the Goulandris-owned Greek Line for $8 million.

A mere eleven months earlier, Greek Line had acquired the 1930-built former Dutch liner, *Johan van Oldenbarnevelt*, which entered their cruise service as the *Lakonia*. She remained with Greek Line for barely eight months, being tragically destroyed by fire while on a Christmas cruise. Greek Line's reputation had not been enhanced by the *Lakonia* from the very outset. Insufficient time had been allotted to her conversion: as a result, when she arrived in Southampton to begin her first Greek Line cruise, she was in chaos. Furthermore, her heavy, darkly-panelled public rooms were woefully outdated and her mixed crew of Greeks, Germans and Italians had little or no understanding of English. Her destruction with over 1,000 passengers aboard only tarnished the Greek Line name further. The acquisition, therefore, of a modern, up-to-date liner to act as a running-mate to their eleven year-old *Olympia* on the Piraeus – New York service would certainly help restore some of the lost lustre to the line. Also, at this time Greek Line needed to face up to the competition that was emerging around them. Under construction was the 25,000 gross ton flagship *Shalom* for the Zim Israel Navigation Company, destined for the Haifa to New York service. In Italy, also in an advanced state of construction were impressive twin flagships for the state-owned Italia company, *Rafaello* and *Michelangelo*. Confidence in trans-Atlantic passenger liners was still running high in the Mediterranean countries, with many emigrant passengers being carried in Tourist Class.

By late April, 1964, both *Empress of England* and *Empress of Canada* had resumed their sailings to the St. Lawrence. Back in European waters, *Empress of Britain* ended her career under the colours of Canadian Pacific with a series of cruises to a whole variety of ports quite new to her. The first of these departed Liverpool on the 11th March for Lisbon, Casablanca and the Atlantic islands and returned to Southampton. Three cruises to Tangier, Gibraltar and Lisbon followed. Then, on the 5th May, she sailed from Liverpool on a 27-day cruise that took her through the Mediterranean to Istanbul and on into the Black Sea to Yalta. She returned via Piraeus, Malta and Lisbon. Between the 1st and 16th June, she cruised to ports in the western Mediterranean. Her next two cruises were something of a departure for a Canadian Pacific ship: on the 18th June, she left Liverpool for the fjords of Norway; and on the 3rd July, she sailed from Southampton for the Baltic ports of Copenhagen, Helsinki and Stockholm. In August, she was again in the Mediterranean: her lucky passengers having the opportunity to explore the French Riviera with the ship at anchor off Monte Carlo on the nights of the 2nd and the 3rd. Her final cruise as *Empress of Britain* departed Southampton on the 13th August and called at Tangier, Gibraltar and Lisbon. She arrived back in Southampton on the 22nd and, having disembarked her passengers, she sailed for Liverpool, arriving there the following day. *Empress of Canada* was in port, discharging cargo and being made ready for another voyage to the St. Lawrence. The careers of these two liners would again cross, and in a most spectacular way, but at that sad time such a thing could not have seemed likely.

Empress of Britain was placed in temporary lay-up, awaiting her delivery to Greek Line. While it was a sad day for British shipping, and particularly for Canadian Pacific who had welcomed her and her sisters with such optimism, for the ship herself it was just the beginning. She had more than proved her versatility, both as an Atlantic liner and as a cruise ship, and over the following decades she would continue doing so.

In August, 1964, Canadian Pacific were seeking to persuade fellow members of the North Atlantic passenger conference to agree to a rise in fares between the United Kingdom and Canada. In reviewing the effect of economy and 21-day excursion fares introduced by airlines on the Atlantic run, it could not be denied that the drain on passenger bookings had increased. Canadian Pacific saw that it was vital that they present a different image in advertising their shipping services. This they had begun to do and they were making strong attempts to infuse a cruise atmosphere into North Atlantic crossings, paying greater attention to entertainment in general. This policy appeared to be paying off. Between the 1st April and the 31st July of that year, the two 'Empresses' had averaged 930 passengers per voyage westbound and 735 eastbound. The corresponding figures for 1963 had been 766 and 665. There were considerable numbers of businessmen flying out to Canada and America who were choosing to return home by ship and Canadian Pacific saw this trend

gradually increasing. The company felt that their sale of *Empress of Britain* earlier in the year had been completely vindicated by the success of the other two liners. In simple fact, if they had still possessed her they would have carried the same number of passengers in three ships instead of two.

The cruise business was seen as more than just a fringe operation. It was vitally important. John Hughes, the company's European passenger manager said: "As far as Canadian Pacific is concerned, we are prepared to stay in the North Atlantic as long as business is profitable, and the same applies to cruising as well. Judging by the present rate of reservations for the 1964/65 cruising season, we have every hope of having full ships: 600-650 for the shorter cruises and 450-500 for the West Indies cruise. These will all be one class." Looking to the future he added: "Demand may well outstrip supply. Canadian Pacific are staying in the passenger business; we are not selling any ship."

On the 17th December, 1964, *Empress of Canada* arrived in New York to begin another season of Caribbean cruises. These were now a well-established part of the New York cruising scene. The most popular was, inevitably, the first cruise of the season. It encompassed both Christmas and New Year and the stay in each port was lengthy, often overnight. On the other side of the Atlantic, *Empress of England* departed Liverpool on the 19th December for a 17-day cruise to Madeira, the Cape Verde Islands, Las Palmas and Gibraltar. She arrived back in Liverpool on the 5th January, 1965, sailing two days later on a magnificent 35-day cruise to the West Indies and the United States. Her ports of call were Casablanca, Las Palmas, Trinidad, Caracas, Jamaica, Port Everglades, Nassau, Barbados and Madeira. She made three further cruises between the 14th February and the 1st April, calling at the more familiar ports in the Canary and Cape Verde Islands, Morocco and Portugal.

As was usual, by mid-April, 1965, the St. Lawrence service was again established. *Empress of England* made her first departure on the 6th April. *Empress of Canada* arrived in the Mersey, from New York, the following day and departed on her first crossing of the season to Canada on the 13th. She made a dramatic exit from the docks, striking the lock wall and damaging plates on both sides of her hull.

Passenger bookings aboard the two 'Empresses' showed a dramatic improvement and the company strove to make their operation more economic. They reduced their turn-around times with the elimination of movements into the Gladstone Dock. It was a sad fact, however, that departures were still sometimes being disrupted by union problems. In July, in an attempt to maintain harmony, *Empress of England* became the first ship to carry seamen's shop stewards and a convenor aboard. Nevertheless, the Canadian Pacific liners would still suffer disruptions to their sailing schedules. *Empress of Canada* continued in the Canadian service through until the 4th November but *Empress of England* had her Atlantic season cut short. She made two late summer/early autumn cruises, her first excursions into the Mediterranean. After that, she made one more sailing over to Canada. It was on this voyage, in the St. Lawrence on the 8th November, that, during a severe snowstorm, she was involved in a collision with a Norwegian tanker. With her bow holed

An impressive gathering: *Empress of England* is seen at Funchal on the 2nd April, 1969 together with the Italian motorliner *Augustus* and the record-breaking *S.S. United States* (far left).
Luis Miguel Correia collection.

Caribbean season, she sailed from New York on the 17th April for Montreal, on her way diverting up the Saguenay River, making her the second largest liner to have sailed up that stretch of water. She passed the steep cliffs of Cape Trinity and Cape Eternity on her way to Port Alfred and Chicoutimi and while she was at Port Alfred a presentation of the flag of the 'Kingdom of Saguenay' was made to the ship. It was a pleasant diversion but, sadly, not one that was a reflection of life aboard her.

The incident that had disrupted her first Atlantic departure from Liverpool in April, 1970 was just one among many. For quite some time, *Empress of Canada* had been plagued with industrial unrest, in particular amongst her stewards who persistently, and totally unacceptably, demanded the use of the passengers' facilities at various times throughout the day while the ship was at sea. In the face of such problems, on top of increased operational costs and dwindling passenger numbers, it had been remarkable that at the time of the withdrawal of *Empress of England*, Canadian Pacific had stressed their determination to keep *Empress of Canada* in service. In fact, rumours had begun to circulate regarding her future and there were even reports that she was available for sale for $8 million. In July, 1971, Canadian Pacific denied that this was true and the ship continued with her regular St. Lawrence sailings.

Then, on the 22nd August, *Empress of Canada* was in the news again. At 8.15 pm, en route from Montreal and one day from arrival in Liverpool, she suffered a blow-back in a boiler which caused a fire in the boiler room. The situation looked serious and there was a full-scale fire alert, with passengers called to the lifeboats and other vessels in the area asked to stand by. In fact, it took her crew just ten minutes to bring the fire under control and the ship arrived in Liverpool only two hours late.

Quite suddenly, a little over two months later, on the 9th November, Canadian Pacific announced that *Empress of Canada* would be withdrawn from service when she arrived back in Liverpool on the 23rd. The mere two weeks notice of her withdrawal doubtless ensured that she ended her service in as dignified a way as was possible, rather than having it marred by unseemly behaviour by her crew. An official statement from Canadian Pacific, quite contrary to the optimistic words spoken by the chairman 14 months earlier, said: "Economic circumstances made it impossible to achieve a viable passenger ship operation." This brought to an end almost two years of rumour and counter-rumour. In 1970, the number of passengers travelling by sea between Britain and Canada had dropped to 23,732 from 98,000 a decade earlier. In addition, *Empress of Canada*'s cruise market was being adversely affected by the relative decline in the value of the U.S. dollar.

With barely 300 passengers aboard, *Empress of Canada* made her final departure from Montreal's Louis Joliet terminal just before 8 am on the 17th November, 1971, with her crew's band playing and singing 'Now is the hour'. She sounded a few long blasts from her siren and was answered by short toots from the tugs. Perhaps, given the early hour, it was not surprising that there were only 20 people on the pier to watch as the two tugs pulled the flag-decked liner into the St. Lawrence before she sailed off into the cold and gloom. It was, nevertheless, sad that so few were there to mark the end of eighty years of 'Empress' tradition and sixty-eight years of passenger service on the North Atlantic. For her part, *Empress of Canada* had completed 121 Atlantic voyages and 82 cruises for the company.

The ship remained in Liverpool until the 14th December, when she was moved to a lay-up berth within London's Tilbury Docks, as there was none suitable for her on the Mersey. Thus, she made her first ever arrival in the Thames on the 17th December. A Canadian Pacific spokesman said that negotiations for her sale were proceeding, with interest being shown by a number of British and foreign companies. However, "one of the difficulties is that, although the ship was built with cruising in mind, the design has since been overtaken by the specialised new 'liners' cruising in both the Mediterranean and the Caribbean."

The once magnificent fleet of Canadian Pacific liners was now but a memory.

Built up at the stern and wearing Greek Line livery, the former _Empress of Britain_ became _Queen Anna Maria_. Here she lies at Piraeus in March, 1965, awaiting the start of her first voyage for her new owners. _Laurence Dunn collection._

6

Queen Anna Maria

Following her sale, *Empress of Britain* was renamed *Queen Anna Maria*. Three painters were called upon to spell out the new name in Greek lettering on her stern. However, because of a misunderstanding, Greek characters were also painted on her bows, instead of the English name as was accepted practice. A sharp-eyed Liverpool docker, on his way home that evening, spotted the mistake and called out to a Greek officer, "That's a funny name on your ship!" The painters had to be hastily recalled and, perched on a platform, they repainted the name in English under the light of arc-lamps.

On the 18th November, 1964, the ship sailed out of the River Mersey for the final time. Her destination was the Mariotti ship repair and conversion facility in Genoa and she arrived there on the 22nd. The work to transform the former British North Atlantic liner into the flagship of Greek Line, for their altogether more cruise-inspired Mediterranean/Atlantic service, began the following day and took three months to complete.

The conversion principally entailed increasing cabin accommodation, creating more open deck space and building an unusually large nightclub of 6,100 sq. feet. The First Class accommodation was left relatively untouched, only a few small changes being made. The cabins on what had been known as A Deck, and was now designated Upper Deck, were increased from 93 to 95 by filling in the space that had been taken up by Number 4 Trunked Hatch. This resulted in an increase in First Class berths from 160 to 168. In the Tourist Class section on the same deck, forward and aft, the number of cabins was increased from 55 to 58, again accomplished by using space from former cargo hatches: Number 5 aft and part of Number 3 forward. Tourist Class berths on this deck now numbered 178, rather than 168.

The main increase in Tourist Class numbers took place on the new A Deck, formerly D Deck, which had previously been used mainly for stores and cargo. Now, instead of just 16 cabins there were 62, all with toilets and showers. On *Empress of Britain* there had been no cabins with private facilities on B, C or D Decks. After her transformation into *Queen Anna Maria*, 452 of her 467 cabins had private facilities. Her total passenger capacity became 1,313 for trans-Atlantic voyages and 742 on cruises. All the passenger accommodation was now fully air-conditioned.

Although the passenger quarters were much changed, very little alteration was made to the rest of the ship. The original steam turbines, giving a speed of 21 knots, were retained and the Denny-Brown stabilisers were not altered.

The skilful conversion did little to change the liner's outward appearance, except at the stern. Here, *Empress of Britain*'s echelon outline gave way to a fully rounded stern on three more decks and the dual rôle of the newly refitted liner, for the North Atlantic run and for cruising, prompted the installation of a remarkable and unique lido

deck. Four pools were created, one in each corner of the new lido. Whilst three of them were very small, the other, set into redundant hatch space on the port side aft, was of more conventional size. Each pool was entirely covered with mosaic tiles, had submerged lighting and varied in depth. One was principally for children and had a small chute; two of the others had taller chutes. The designers felt that four smaller pools had distinct advantages over one big one: they lent themselves to better variety of design, they precluded the movement of a big volume of water in swells and they had the novelty that swimmers could go from pool to pool at random. Forward of the lido pools was an open-air verandah bar, originally a Tourist Class promenade on the Boat Deck. Forward of this again, amidships, was a raised sports deck area. Thus, the designers of the conversion created a sports area at different levels, from the aftermost point of the ship to the funnel. The original indoor swimming pool was also retained.

Refinements below decks included an extension of the hospital area and the addition of a gymnasium, sauna bath and rest room adjoining the indoor pool, in space previously used for food storage. Reflecting the fact that Haifa would feature prominently in the sailing schedules, a small synagogue was built on the Promenade Deck, once again using former hatch space, and a separate kosher restaurant for 74 people now adjoined the First Class restaurant. This was created in space that had previously been taken up by twelve Tourist Class cabins. Two extra bar service counters were added to lounges on the Promenade Deck and a photographer's shop was installed in what was previously a hatchway.

As built, *Empress of Britain* was a luxurious ship of the finest kind. However, the skilful conversion planned by Greek Line engineers gave her even greater cruising potential. They enhanced her considerably by extending the air-conditioning to all of the cabins and public rooms and by installing private bathrooms to virtually all cabins – which by that time was obligatory in prestige passenger liners, particularly those whose principal market was the United States. Further improvement came from the installation of the extensive lido and the large night club. Now, she was a match to all the new tonnage then being built and, at barely nine years, she was herself still a comparatively new ship. Once more, it was fitting that she should take the rôle of flagship.

However, her overall character remained the same, despite all the changes. The essentially British-styled North Atlantic liner décor remained intact. The tiered aft decks, of course, had all been extended to the stern to allow for the creation of the vast new night club and this somewhat compromised her low and elegant lines, but the new structure was thoughtfully designed and graceful in its own way. Its full-length windows, of the same proportions as those along the promenade, wrapped around the stern, giving the impression that it was the original structure

An aerial view shows the huge lido and sports deck areas which the ship acquired during her skilful conversion by the Mariotti company of Genoa. *Laurence Dunn collection.*

rather than a newer addition. Unfortunately, the same could not be said of its decorative style. Although it became a very popular room, its sterile décor and angular 'airport lounge'-style furnishings contrasted sharply with the glossy panelling and solid comfort of the rest of the ship.

Queen Anna Maria emerged fresh from her refit on the 6th March, 1965, proudly carrying the handsome Greek Line livery on her funnel: a yellow base, a broad blue band around its centre and a black top, with a golden trident device displayed on the blue band. It was, without doubt, the most attractive of the many funnel colours that this liner would wear during her career. Although Greek Line belonged to the Goulandris Group, the ownership of the vessel was officially with the splendidly named Transoceanic Navigation Corporation of Monrovia. Just to confuse the issue even further, she was Greek registered, at Andros, located on the island of the same name in the Cyclades group. Although she now presented a somewhat more built-up profile, her tonnage was revised downwards, according to Greek standards: instead of being 25,516 gross tons, she was now listed as 21,716 gross tons.

The 'new' flagship steamed into Piraeus harbour on the 9th March, 1965. Finishing touches were made to her and she was readied to begin her second career. On the 15th, Their Majesties King Constantine and Queen Anna Maria were welcomed aboard by the officials of the company. The liner was to be given a unique distinction: Queen Anna Maria, in whose honour she had been named, had been asked to perform the naming ceremony. This took place in the Tourist Class lounge and the young Queen unveiled a plaque to commemorate the occasion. Thus, the liner became the only one ever to have been named by two reigning queens.

Four days later, *Queen Anna Maria* departed Piraeus on her first voyage under the Greek Line flag. She had as her master Captain John Polychroniades, a seaman with a most distinguished 26-year career. He was a Rear Admiral in the Greek Royal Naval Reserve and held the Order of the Phoenix (Commander Class), as well as the order of St. George and ten other decorations, including the French Légion d'Honneur, awarded for his services during the War. As a captain in the Greek merchant marine, he had commanded vessels of up to 50,000 gross tons in South Atlantic, West African, Mediterranean and Black Sea services. He was also an accomplished linguist, speaking English, French, Italian and Arabic, skills that made him well-suited to the rôle of master of the new Greek Line flagship.

That first voyage of *Queen Anna Maria* was in effect a four-day cruise and took her to Haifa. She was back in Piraeus on the 23rd and on the following day she departed for New York. Even her most regular route had an itinerary that read more like a cruise. Having departed Piraeus, she called at Naples, Palermo and Lisbon: this took five days even before she headed out across the Atlantic. (There was still a large market for passengers on this route, especially travelling Tourist Class, primarily emigrants, not only from Greece but also from Italy and Portugal.) Once across the Atlantic, she made a call at Halifax, Nova Scotia before finally arriving in New York on the 5th April. The Mayor of New York, John Lindsay, proclaimed it Queen Anna Maria Day in honour of the ship. Her return voyage began on the 7th and called at the

same ports, with the exception of Halifax which was only included on westbound voyages. Sometimes, she would call at other ports, as was the case after that first return crossing. Having arrived back in Piraeus on the 18th April, she sailed again on the 21st and arrived in Istanbul on the 22nd, departing from there the following day for Haifa. It was while she was there that she had the misfortune to foul one of her propellers. She was, however, able to continue her voyage next day. Back in Piraeus on the 28th, she sailed later that day for New York. On her return to the Mediterranean, she included calls at Valetta in Malta and Limassol in Cyprus and from then onward Limassol featured often in her schedules.

The year 1965 was a significant one with regard to Mediterranean-based Atlantic passenger services. After *Queen Anna Maria*'s introduction by the Greek Line in March, the magnificent new twin flagships of Italia, *Michelangelo* and *Raffaello*, entered service on the 12th May and the 25th July, respectively. The Italian fleet was a force to be reckoned with as the two new liners joined the already well-established *Leonardo da Vinci* and *Cristoforo Colombo* on the New York run. Zim Lines had taken delivery of their new flagship *Shalom* the previous April and the American Export Line's *Independence*, *Constitution* and *Atlantic* were also powerful competitors on the New York to the Mediterranean service. It was some measure of the charm and welcoming ambience aboard the still very British-styled *Queen Anna Maria* that she was able to compete successfully against these more glamorous and stylish rivals. Until the arrival of *Queen Anna Maria*, Greek Line had maintained their service on the route with just one ship, the 22,979 gross ton *Olympia*. The rival National Hellenic American Line, a Greek flag subsidiary of Home Lines, had been running the aged but still popular *Queen Frederica*. However, at the end of 1965, Home Lines withdrew from the trade, selling the National Hellenic American Line and its ship to Chandris, who mainly used her for cruises and emigrant sailings to Australia, with only a few voyages to America.

All of these liners on the trans-Atlantic route from the Mediterranean ports were operated on extensive cruise-like itineraries. These were very popular with many American passengers, who would actually board the ships for the round trip, as an extended cruise. In fact, this was seen as being a very lucrative business and the shipping lines were anxious to promote this aspect of their services.

Queen Anna Maria's terminal port in the Mediterranean was Haifa, in Israel, and a typical round voyage would be of twenty-eight days duration. She maintained her first season on the route until the end of November, arriving in New York on the 29th. Later that same day, she sailed on her first Caribbean cruise for Greek Line, calling at Curaçao, St. Thomas and San Juan. On the 12th December, she sailed again for the Mediterranean: on this occasion her voyage ended in Piraeus, where she arrived on the 23rd. She remained there until the 8th January, 1966, when she left for New York but on this occasion her route was via Messina, Palermo, Naples, Genoa and Halifax. Once into the Atlantic, it was a typical wintertime crossing and during the 16th, 17th and 18th she encountered heavy weather and sustained some damage as a result. This necessitated repairs to 20 feet of bulwarks; and 30 feet of teak rail at the forward end of the promenade deck needed renewing.

More seriously, her foremast had to be straightened and four Carley floats and some cargo handling gear had to be renewed.

On the 21st January, she sailed on her second cruise, once again to the more welcoming and placid waters of the Caribbean. It was a thirteen-day trip calling at Port au Prince, Cartagena, Cristobal, Kingston and Nassau. She was back in New York on the 3rd February. The following morning, as she was being prepared to embark her next passengers, her former fleetmate *Empress of Canada* berthed nearby. It was the first time they had been in port together since, as *Empress of Britain*, *Queen Anna Maria* had arrived in Liverpool for the last time as a Canadian Pacific liner. However, despite their diverse careers, the two ships were destined to meet several times more. On the 4th, *Queen Anna Maria* sailed on one of her more extended Mediterranean voyages – forty-four days that would include additional calls at Tangier, Alexandria, Istanbul, Messina, Cannes, Barcelona, Palma and Majorca. It was, perhaps, an indication of her status as the flagship that she undertook just three cruises that winter, Greek Line preferring to maintain her on the Mediterranean/Atlantic service. Meanwhile, her fleetmate *Olympia* operated six cruises down to the Caribbean, one 5-day trip to Bermuda and a 3-night 'cruise to nowhere'.

Queen Anna Maria continued her Mediterranean sailings throughout the summer of 1966. A deviation from her usual routine came on the 21st October, when she left New York on a three-night 'cruise to nowhere'. It was the first time she had made such a trip but these brief, 'get away from it all' cruises would in future become a popular fixture in her sailing schedules. On the 21st December, she was once again berthed near to *Empress of Canada* in New York and the following day both liners departed on cruises to the Caribbean. Several days later they were in St. Thomas together. Their cruises ended on the same day, so once more they were in New York side by side and again, on the 7th January, 1967, they were in St. Thomas together. Then on the 23rd January, there was another sisterly reunion when *Queen Anna Maria* shared her berth in Kingston, Jamaica with *Empress of England*.

Over that 1966/67 winter, *Queen Anna Maria* undertook five cruises from New York to the Caribbean. The final one was to be unfortunately memorable. On the 19th February, while arriving at Kingston, she ran aground at 7 am near St. Albans Beacon and became stuck fast. An inspection revealed that she was grounded on her starboard side for about 270 feet of her length and, when it became clear that all efforts to refloat her were unsuccessful, her 665 passengers were disembarked, with arrangements being made to have them flown home. Eventually, it was agreed that a dredger should clear the area where she was aground. When this was done, her bunkers were off-loaded. Then, at noon on the 26th, she was finally freed and proceeded to an anchorage where she could be inspected by divers. Despite having been aground for a week, she showed no evidence of damage and she was able to sail for New York on the 27th, her schedule now in some disarray.

Greek Line had originally planned for her to make a call at Port Everglades on the 21st, to disembark and embark passengers, and then continue up to New York. From there, she was to sail on what had been promoted as her Mediterranean and Greek Islands Royal Diadem

Cruises: forty-six days, calling at nineteen ports and eleven countries. While she was firmly aground off Jamaica, Greek Line had hastily to reschedule the cruise. Now, she sailed on the 3rd March, calling at Tangier, Valetta, Heraklion, Alexandria and Haifa. A scheduled call at Rhodes had been abandoned and she continued up to Istanbul for an overnight stop and then down to Piraeus. *Queen Anna Maria* was there on the 23rd and 24th March and sailed the following day. However, the best-laid plans were once again put to the test when she was forced to return to Piraeus with mechanical problems. She sailed again on the 27th but the calls at Syracuse, Messina, Alghero and Gibraltar all had to be dropped from the itinerary. Nevertheless, she still visited her more regular ports of Naples, Cannes and Lisbon before returning to New York. It had been an eventful two months and doubtless a fretful time for Greek Line staff.

Fortunately, the remainder of 1967 passed without incident. On the 8th September, the schedule of Atlantic crossings was again interrupted by a three-night 'cruise to nowhere' out of New York. Ship enthusiast and regular cruise passenger Denny Bond Beattie, Jnr. was aboard:

"I saw the *Queen Anna Maria* on her first arrival under the Greek Line flag and at that time remarked that she was fundamentally still Canadian Pacific in atmosphere, with the addition of the nightclub and lido deck area. I had been on her sister ship *Empress of England* at least ten years before, when they were both new and doing West Indies cruise service out of New York in the wintertime. I had the chance to sample this ship" (i.e. – *Queen Anna Maria*) "on a weekend 'cruise to nowhere' with a group of 15, sailing at 6.30 pm, Friday 8th September. Embarkation started at 3.30 pm. Typical of New York – everyone loves to come to a sailing party – even for so short a cruise. Sometimes a longer cruise sails at an hour at which few can come but late Friday afternoon was perfect to gather a large crowd. We had the portion of the Zacharatos Lounge opposite the Dolphin Bar for our party, complete with champagne and handled by Sam (as we called him), one of the bar stewards. After we sailed, Sam seemed to be everywhere and we continued to have good service from him. On Saturday night, he set up a Pre-Dinner cocktail party for 30 people for us, and it was well done. The departure was as gay as for any longer cruise and we headed majestically out to sea. I shared stateroom M81 – amidships, outside – with our own 'cruise director' and organiser. A comfortable room with bed, convertible sofa, easy chair and bench, plus bathroom. This cabin became our 'hospitality room', which always adds to the trip.

"Our group, of 15, had two long tables for 10 in the dining room – 8 on one and 7 on the other. The line found it necessary to add three single people to one table – which worked out well – and we could eat at either table. We were in second sitting and had two excellent waiters. Only the main dining room was used: the normal First Class Dining Room was not used at all – nor was the special Tourist Class Kosher Dining Room. The menu offered a great selection and basically everything was very good. It was not Cordon Bleu gourmet but then you must remember that they were serving 800 at two sittings with a First Class menu and, considering everything, I had no complaints, and I did sample a lot. However, typical of a foreign ship, you don't get a good American breakfast – especially eggs.

With an all-white hull and the Greek Line crest on her bow, *Queen Anna Maria* **was both a trans-Atlantic liner and a notable cruise ship.** *Luís Miguel Correia collection.*

"The ship had three orchestras aboard – one Greek, one Italian and one American – playing for dancing or cocktail music. I thought the Greek orchestra the best. There were three variety shows – one each night – plus the usual Bingo, horse racing and Greek dancing instruction.

"Saturday was the most beautiful day at sea and the lido was well used. Our group had ten deck chairs in a row (for 15 – which worked out well). We sampled the four outdoor pools – including the slides! The usual lifeboat drill had been held at 10.15 that morning.

"The Promenade Deck, port side, was set up with tables and chairs for 11 am bouillon and crackers, afternoon tea and 11 pm buffet. I did look in on all of these but only sampled the bouillon one morning. I never did see any trays of hors d'oeuvres served at cocktail time: only bowls of nuts and pretzels. There was no reception or Captain's Cocktail Party for passengers. This had been done on previous Greek Line weekend cruises. These are usually mob scenes but you do get a free drink and a

chance to meet the Captain.

"Of the public rooms, I thought the Olympian Ballroom the nicest for dancing. I didn't think much of the Nightclub, except to enjoy its bar during the day – it is right at the stern. Speaking of bars, the Athenian Bar, forward, seemed to be a favourite spot of mine as well as the surrounding Garden Lounge. This was an excellent place to enjoy Greek Metaxas brandy after dinner, for 30 cents. I did try Ouzo, which is like Pernod, and costs 20 cents. Another bargain, for 10 cents, was a cup of Italian demi-tasse coffee from a huge pressure coffee machine.

"Sunday was cloudy and overcast and with some rain. Later, we were racing to New York to get away from Hurricane Doria. However, there is much diversion on board ship and a cloudy day need not interfere. We had arranged an engine room tour for 10 that morning – which was very complete – starting from the Engineer Officer's quarters on Boat Deck and going down in the private elevator to the engine room and working back along the

Although the alterations to her stern deprived _Queen Anna Maria_ of some of her former elegance, they were done with sensitivity, particularly in the configuration of the windows. _Luís Miguel Correia collection._

twin screw shafts.

"In lieu of outdoor swimming, we used the indoor pool, with its gym and sauna. The latter two are new on the _Queen Anna Maria_. The pool water was very warm and the sauna not as hot as on Swedish ships: but still, I was glad these were available for use.

"The farewell Dinner was excellent, with fine food and a Baked Alaska served flaming to all tables at one time – a take-off on the famed Swedish American Line Farewell Dinner, to which none can compare. However, this did add a fine touch to the evening and, typical of any dessert course, our steward still wanted to bring us slices of watermelon and other melons, as he had done at previous meals.

"We docked on Monday morning at 8 am and I was at work before 9 – completely satisfied. This was a fine cruise."

Queen Anna Maria resumed her Atlantic schedule after this brief cruise, on the 11th September, making three further round trip voyages to the Mediterranean. On the 22nd December, 1967, she departed New York on the first

of a series of nine cruises to the Caribbean. It was her most extensive cruise programme so far, under the Greek Line flag, and it was an indication of the way in which the ocean liner market was beginning to change. At that time, most of the cruises for the American market were from the port of New York and these trips were no exception. But two of them, of nine and of ten days duration, called at just one port: St. Thomas. Such cruises, although in many cases from Miami, would in time become the mainstay of the American cruise market.

On her return to the Mediterranean for the 1968 trans-Atlantic season, the ship suffered boiler damage while at Haifa on the 12th April. The necessary repairs extended her stay until the 15th. Normally, she arrived there in the morning and left that same evening. The rest of her Atlantic service for that year continued without disruption, except for two 'cruises to nowhere, on the 6th-7th June and in November. This would, however, be _Queen Anna Maria_'s final virtually uninterrupted season as a trans-Atlantic liner. On the 19th December, she arrived in New York and was made ready for a further series of winter cruises to the Caribbean. The following day, as her passengers were beginning to embark, she once again encountered *Empress of Canada*, which was making her first arrival in the new CP Ships livery. They met again a few weeks later, on the 7th January, 1969, when they were both anchored off St. Thomas. Then, on the 18th January, there was a reunion between *Queen Anna Maria* and *Empress of England* at Port of Spain in Trinidad.

On the 19th March, having completed her final Caribbean cruise of the 1968-69 season, *Queen Anna Maria* sailed again for the Mediterranean. On the 11th July, while she was en route for Halifax and New York, it was necessary for her to put into Gibraltar as she was suffering from damage to her bearings. The repairs were made by her crew and she was able to sail later that same day. She arrived at New York on the 18th. However, by that time, Greek Line were beginning to see that, even at what had been considered the very height of the trans-Atlantic season, it was far more lucrative to divert their flagship to further cruising. Both she and her fleet mate *Olympia* had developed a loyal following of cruise passengers.

A series of four 6-night cruises from New York to Bermuda had been planned for *Queen Anna Maria*, from the 19th July to the 15th August. On that day, she sailed on a two-night 'cruise to nowhere' before making one more round trip to the Mediterranean. She was back in New York by the end of October, her Atlantic sailings at an end for the year. Again, she turned to Caribbean cruising, this time through to the 6th April, 1970.

Between the 6th April and the end of July, she made four round trips across the Atlantic, interspersed in June and July with two further 'cruises to nowhere'. During August and September, four cruises were made to Bermuda and one voyage to the Mediterranean. There was also another 'cruise to nowhere'. Sailings to Bermuda continued, although from the 10th to the 16th October she cruised to Nassau instead. After one final Mediterranean voyage, *Queen Anna Maria* finished 1970 with a Christmas cruise to Freeport, in the Bahamas. This was the first of six such cruises, some being rather more extensive and sailing deeper into the Caribbean. Three of them departed from Boston rather than New York.

Queen Anna Maria's first trans-Atlantic sailing of 1971 left New York on the 20th April. It was a twenty-six day round trip voyage as far as Haifa. By the 15th May she was back in New York and ready to undertake four further cruises. Once again, they were based on Boston: they were of six and seven days duration, calling principally at Bermuda but one of them was to St. Thomas and another called at Nassau and Freeport. Then, on the 12th June, she made an overnight cruise from New York before setting out once more for the Mediterranean. Back again in New York on the 9th July, she made another 'cruise to nowhere', this time of two nights duration, before starting a further voyage across the Atlantic. When she returned to New York on the 6th August, she embarked upon more cruises on the New York – Bermuda run, each giving her passengers four days and three nights to explore this lovely island. During September, she made a further voyage to Greece and Israel, her only other call on this trip being at Messina. Then it was briefly back to cruising, with two of her cruises being from Philadelphia, her first calls at this port.

On the 28th October, *Queen Anna Maria* departed again for the Mediterranean. Although this voyage took in Malta, Messina and Naples, as well as her usual calls at Piraeus and Haifa, her more diverse routing through the Mediterranean had been dropped in an attempt to remain viable. Her final Mediterranean port on the return voyage was Naples on the 14th November: from there she steamed direct for New York, arriving on the 23rd. She was then employed on an extensive series of cruises through until the 16th April, 1972. Most of them were from New York but some were from Boston. They were mainly to the Caribbean but a few were to the Bahamas – plus the usual 'cruise to nowhere'.

Greek Line worked both their liners, *Queen Anna Maria* and *Olympia*, very hard. During the remainder of 1972, *Queen Anna Maria* made four Atlantic/Mediterranean voyages. They were interspersed with cruises down to the Caribbean, the Bahamas and Bermuda as before. However, in August, she twice headed northwards to Nova Scotia and along the St. Lawrence, the first cruise including a call at Quebec and the second also visiting Montreal. It was the first time in nine years that she had been in those once familiar waters.

Queen Anna Maria sailed from New York on her final Atlantic voyage of the year on the 6th November. She arrived in Piraeus on the 23rd November, remaining there until the 4th December, undergoing overhaul and refitting work. Her return to New York turned out to be one of her final liner voyages, and it was somewhat eventful. She had to make an unscheduled call at Palermo on the 6th for temporary repairs to a damaged port main turbine. Then, on the 14th, when in mid-Atlantic, she encountered heavy weather and as a result sustained some damage to her forward deck equipment. However, she was back in New York in time to make a Christmas and New Year cruise to St. Thomas and Antigua. Early in January, 1973, she again suffered turbine problems, this time with the starboard unit, and a turbine expert had to be flown out to St. Thomas to carry out an inspection. Her high-pressure rotor was removed and sent by air-freight to Hoboken, N.J., for repairs. *Queen Anna Maria*, having been restored to health, sailed from New York on a brief trial voyage on the 24th, returning the same day and resuming her schedule on the 25th. After the programme of Caribbean cruises, she made several more to Bermuda and the Bahamas and again cruised up to Quebec and Montreal – making three such trips that year.

Greek Line had held on to maintaining some semblance of an Atlantic service for as long as possible. However, doing so was a drain on the finances of the already troubled company. The only other line now operating a regular service between the Mediterranean and New York was the once-mighty Italia, by this time reduced to just three liners, albeit the magnificent *Michelangelo*, *Raffaello* and *Leonardo da Vinci*: and even they were spending more time cruising than on Atlantic crossings. The wake of the great ocean liners across the Atlantic had been all but replaced by the vapour trails of jet airliners in the sky. Thus, the directors at Greek Line had acknowledged that if they were to remain in business it had to be as operators of cruise ships rather than trans-Atlantic liners. Fortunately, both *Queen Anna Maria* and *Olympia* had been designed with cruising in mind: in fact, in 1970 *Olympia* had undergone an extensive refit that brought her fully up to the expected cruise ship standards of the day. It has been said that this refit cheapened her and that certain aspects of the décor of both ships, such as brown shag-pile carpets and orange or gold velvet bedspreads, made them resemble budget hotels. But both had become very successful cruise ships and had developed enviable reputations as happy, friendly vessels.

The 'nowhere' cruises were so popular that they were often over-booked and the two running mates became known as 'the good time ships'. The party mood aboard was very high. Greek Line had therefore decided to capitalise on this and ran an extensive programme of cruises out of both New York and Boston throughout 1973. From the late summer of that year through until mid-March, 1974, *Olympia* and *Queen Anna Maria* made some twenty-three cruises to Bermuda and the Caribbean, all different itineraries. They ranged in duration from 4 to 15 days and, on one gala trip or another, included stopovers at 16 ports from Bermuda to Panama. Greek Line even made a deal with developers in Freeport in the Bahamas at about this time – the area was then in the throes of development and both ships called there quite often, with passengers even attending a sales pitch for time-shares.

Queen Anna Maria had embarked on her only trans-Atlantic voyage of 1973 when she sailed from New York on the 5th November bound for Piraeus and her annual overhaul. She remained there until the 12th January, 1974, a Christmas and New Year cruise not having been scheduled for her that year. The Greek Line directors had, however, been looking at the way in which the cruise market had been developing. Several new, purpose-built ships were beginning to enter service in the Caribbean, geared to the 7-day fly-cruise market. They were proving very successful. Another factor that every shipowner had to confront at that time was the dramatic increase in fuel oil costs. Greek Line therefore decided to experiment with the fly-cruise concept and they planned a series of winter cruises for *Queen Anna Maria* based in San Juan, Puerto Rico, with passengers being flown out to join the ship already in the Caribbean . When she left Piraeus on the 12th January, therefore, it was for San Juan rather than for New York.

This programme of 7-day fly-cruises lasted until mid-March. Then, from the 20th, she was based in Baltimore for a series of cruises to Bermuda, the Bahamas and St. Thomas. A similar programme followed out of Philadelphia but unfortunately by now things were looking very bleak for Greek Line – and indeed for many other shipping companies. Greek Line had already been experiencing financial difficulties but things were made even worse when their new venture, to position *Olympia* in the Aegean for cruises around the islands, had to be cancelled. The increases in fuel costs would cut into the projected passenger loads (because of the rise they were causing in air fares from the United States, which had been expected to produce the majority of her passengers). Fuel prices would also affect her own operational costs. Reluctantly, Greek Line withdrew *Olympia* from service and placed her in what was expected to be temporary lay-up. She would, in fact, remain there for over seven years.

Meanwhile, *Queen Anna Maria* attempted to soldier on, sailing from Norfolk, Virginia, but the spectre of bankruptcy was looming. On the 10th June, ship enthusiast Hall Coons, then just a fifteen year-old boy, boarded the ship with his family for a four-day cruise to Nassau. The careworn state of the Greek Line flagship did little to impress him. In fact, *United States*, which was berthed nearby and had been inactive for five years, still appeared to him to be in better condition.

"I remember thinking, gosh, I wish we could sail on the *United States*. The *Queen Anna Maria* looked very dowdy in comparison, with quite a lot of rust on her hull, especially round her anchor. Upon boarding the ship, we were also disappointed in her overall style. The cabins were small and strangely laid out. Going on deck, we were aghast at the brightly coloured and very small pools.

"While the food and the service were very good, the dining room was rather crowded and noisy. The former First Class dining room was not being used and seemed to have been out of action for years. My major memory of the public lounges is that most of the furniture was covered in a bland green fabric and there was a lot of dark wood and an overall gloomy décor, which did not seem to suit our Nassau cruise.

"During the first full day at sea, the alarm bells went off and we saw the crew in the area of our cabin running around with life jackets on. The friends of my parents with whom we had sailed became very scared, as they thought the ship was sinking. Of course, it turned out to be a boat drill but, with typical Greek Line efficiency, they had not bothered to inform the passengers ahead of time. We were supposed to have one day in Nassau but on our arrival there no one could leave the ship, as the Greek Line officials could not get permission from the port authorities for the passengers to disembark. Although we had docked at 9 am, no one got off until noon.

"On our return to Norfolk, the ship developed a very strong vibration in the lounge at the stern of the ship. Everything shook so much that the show that was to be held in the room that evening had to be cancelled. Arriving back in Norfolk, we again had a long wait before we could disembark. We were glad to be home and vowed we would never sail with the Greeks again."

Indeed, the opportunity for anyone to sail again with Greek Line was fast vanishing. *Queen Anna Maria* was still popular, even against the competition of the newer ships, and she managed to sail at around 80% capacity on most of her cruises. But the increased cost of operating her, notably the continually rising price of fuel, became a burden Greek Line were finding it difficult to bear, although they remained optimistic that they would be able to ride out the difficult times. As though to add to the gloom, on the 1st November, when returning from an 11-day Caribbean cruise, the ship ran aground in the Delaware River. Fortunately, with the aid of tugs, she was refloated four hours later, undamaged. As an indication of her popularity, she had 655 passengers aboard for that cruise. She managed to struggle on under the increasing burden of debts, but by now she was only sailing sporadically, with periods of lay-up, sometimes for as much as two or three weeks at a time.

In those early years of the 1970s, Greek Line was not alone in its struggle to remain viable in the face of escalating operational costs. Many well-known liners and cruise ships were making a one-way voyage to the breakers' yards in the Far East. However, it seems that

Greek Line had lost its vigour and momentum a few years earlier, after the death of its owner and chairman, Basil Goulandris. Although the company was based in Greece, Mr. Goulandris, with all the flair and panache one would expect of a Greek shipping magnate, lived in a suite in London's prestigious Claridge's Hotel. It was from there that, with his innate understanding of the shipping world, he developed the line into the great success that it had become by the time he acquired the former *Empress of Britain* and transformed her into the equally successful *Queen Anna Maria*. Regrettably, in the years following his death, Greek Line seemed to lose its way. The rapid increase in the price of fuel oil in 1973 was the final blow for an already ailing line.

For 1974-75, a 13-day Christmas cruise had been scheduled, along with two Grand Slam cruises of 15 and 13 days, a 13-night wine-themed Bacchus cruise and a 14-night Gala Mid-Winter cruise calling at seven Caribbean ports. A 10-night Passover cruise had also been announced. However, *Queen Anna Maria*'s cruise from Baltimore to Bermuda starting on the 25th November,

1974 proved to be her last under the Greek Line flag. She was back in Baltimore on the 2nd December, her career with Greek Line at an end: in fact, Greek Line itself was at an end as its debts had continued to mount up. *Queen Anna Maria* was moved to a temporary lay-up berth in Hampton Roads but then, on the 20th December, she was berthed in New York. It was the first time she had arrived there that year.

She had been scheduled to leave on the 18th January on a cruise to the Caribbean and Bermuda. However, in a statement issued on behalf of her owners, Transoceanic Navigation Corporation, it was announced that the sailing was cancelled, along with the balance of the 1975 season. The reason was frankly stated: "financial difficulties which had made it impossible for the ship owners to continue with the cruise programme". During the cold days of early 1975, with the official announcement of the collapse of the Greek Line's entire passenger division, it became apparent to the creditors that Transoceanic's only asset was tied up at a Manhattan pier. They made arrangements to seize her. However, forewarned that this was about to happen,

The trans-Atlantic voyages of *Queen Anna Maria*, the 'glamorous flagship of the Greek Line', were also marketed as cruises along the 'Royal Diadem route'. *Author's collection.*

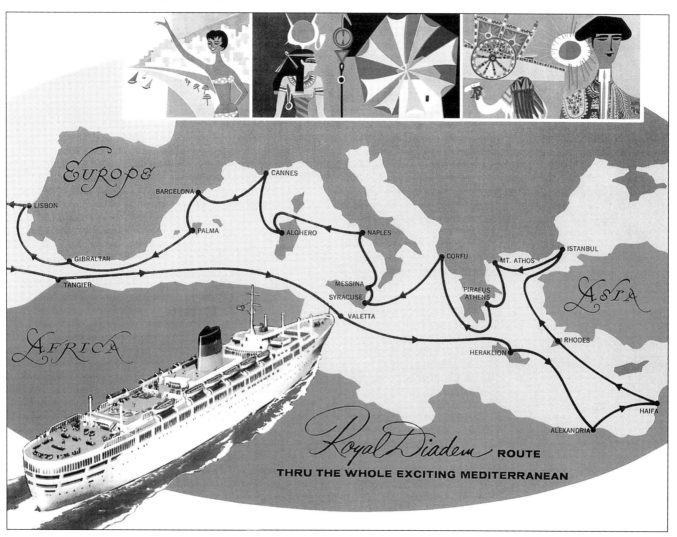

her crew made her ready for a quick and unannounced departure on the 11th January. It was a particularly ignominious farewell to a port that had once welcomed her by proclaiming a day in her honour. The Chase Manhattan Bank, who held the mortgage on the ship, had provided the money for the fuel needed to sail her to Greece. It seems that in the United States, Chase Manhattan would have had less leverage in bankruptcy proceedings whereas in Greece they could take possession of the ship.

She passed Gibraltar on the 18th and arrived in Piraeus on the 22nd. Mr. John Goulandris, a director of Ormos Shipping, the general agents for Transocean Navigation, confirmed on the 20th that *Queen Anna Maria* would be laid up. He also admitted that the owning companies of both *Queen Anna Maria* and *Olympia* were in grave financial troubles. "The *Queen Anna Maria* had been programmed for a whole series of cruises up to the end of the year, but I understand that ticket sales were not progressing satisfactorily enough and the company reached a point where it could not afford to carry on," he said. *Queen Anna Maria*'s days as the elegant flagship of Greek Line were over and she was laid up, along with many other redundant liners, in Perama.

With the collapse of her owners in 1975, *Queen Anna Maria* was laid up at Perama, close to the former Typaldos ferry *Hania*, once the Bibby passenger/cargo liner *Warwickshire*. *Luís Miguel Correia collection.*

7
Ocean Monarch

Within only a few days of Canadian Pacific announcing in January, 1970 that they intended to withdraw *Empress of England* from their service on the 1st April, she was purchased for £5 million by Shaw Savill Line (Shaw, Savill & Albion Co., Ltd.) There had not even been time to announce formally that she was available for sale. In fact, this ranked as being one of the fastest such deals ever recorded. Such was the reputation of *Empress of Britain* and *Empress of England*, that both had found willing buyers very quickly. Commenting on the acquisition of the ship, Mr. Bob Russell, chairman of Shaw Savill, said: "When the *Empress of England* became available, we decided immediately that she would be a most satisfactory partner to join *Northern Star* and *Southern Cross* in our extremely popular Round-the-World service and that is why we moved in quickly and bought her." He went on to confirm that the company intended to carry out some modifications to her and that she would also undertake cruises from both the United Kingdom and Australia.

On the 4th April, *Empress of England* was renamed *Ocean Monarch*. At that time, there was still considerable ocean liner traffic on the routes to Australia and New Zealand and Shaw Savill, buoyed with optimism for the future success of this market, were expanding their passenger fleet. Both *Southern Cross* and *Northern Star* were well-established on their Round-the-World service (although *Northern Star* never acquired quite the same degree of popularity as her older sister). In 1969, the beautiful Royal Mail liners *Amazon*, *Aragon* and *Arlanza*, unable to pay their way on the United Kingdom to Argentina service, were transferred within the Furness Withy group to Shaw Savill. Renamed *Akaroa*, *Aranda* and *Arawa* respectively, they also went into service out to Australia and New Zealand. Given that back in the early 1950s the company had seen that there was no future in combining passengers and cargo – hence the development of the highly popular passengers-only *Southern Cross* – it appeared a curious decision. Certainly, it was an unfortunate one. Together with *Ceramic*, the company's last remaining member of the previous generation of cargo/passenger ships, and *Southern Cross* and *Northern Star*, they formed one of the largest British deep-sea passenger fleets, with over 4,000 one-class tourist berths at their disposal. The arrival of *Ocean Monarch* pushed this figure up to over 5,000.

On the 11th April, 1970, less than two weeks after she had completed her final cruise for Canadian Pacific, and looking little different except for the new name at her bows and stern and her newly painted black-topped buff funnel, *Ocean Monarch* sailed from Liverpool on her first voyage for Shaw Savill. This was to Australia via South Africa. She called at Las Palmas, then Cape Town and Durban – ports that she had last visited while under charter to the TSA – before setting off across the Indian Ocean to Fremantle, Melbourne and Sydney. She arrived in Sydney on the 15th May and departed on a 39-day cruise on the

17th. At this time, a World Expo was being held in Japan and Shaw Savill were marketing two cruises enabling *Ocean Monarch*'s passengers to experience the event, as well as visit other exciting oriental cities. After a brief call at Brisbane to embark more passengers, she steamed non-stop for Japan, arriving in Yokohama on the 29th after giving her passengers nine whole days at sea. She remained at Yokohama until the 31st, when she sailed for Kobe for a further two-night stay. Homeward, she called at Hong Kong from the 7th to the 9th June. On the 13th and the 14th, she was in Singapore before leaving for Fremantle, Melbourne and Sydney.

The second of these cruises to Japan was of a mere 28 days and called at Manila on the homeward journey rather than going round the western coast of Australia. There followed an eight-day cruise across the Tasman Sea to New Zealand, starting on the 2nd August and calling at Wellington and Auckland. Then, on the 11th August, *Ocean Monarch* embarked passengers for a liner voyage back to the United Kingdom, again via South Africa.

While *Ocean Monarch* was being successfully introduced into the Shaw Savill fleet, plans were being drawn up to give her a £2 million refit that would bring her more into line with the demands of her new service. A seven-man team from Cammell Laird (Ship Repairers), Ltd. had embarked at Las Palmas and, as the ship voyaged towards Southampton, had made preliminary studies for the planned seven month conversion to be carried out at their Birkenhead yard. Mr. William Cooke, project manager, said that he thought the single largest job would be the stripping out of crew cabins and decks and the building of crew quarters elsewhere, while erecting new passenger accommodation in the areas formerly used by the crew. "The conversion is an extremely big job and has to be carried out in a comparatively short time. I would say that our chances of improving on the time schedule are slim compared with our chances of over-running it," he said, not knowing just how prophetic his statement would be.

Having disembarked her passengers at Southampton on the 15th September, *Ocean Monarch* sailed the following day for the Mersey and the Birkenhead shipyard. She was scheduled to return to service with a cruise departing from Southampton on the 23rd April, 1971. Unfortunately, the refit was beset with problems, labour unrest and strikes. The work dragged on and Shaw Savill were faced with the embarrassment of having to reschedule, and then cancel, seven of the eight cruises they had planned for the ship that year. It was estimated that as a result they lost £12 million in revenue; and the final cost of the refit had risen to £4 million. It can have been of little comfort to know that Cammell Laird themselves lost £1¼ million on the conversion, due to their underestimation of the cost of the work. In the end, Shaw Savill forfeited the goodwill of many of their passengers and Cammell Laird had their reputation considerably tarnished as well.

The former *Empress of England*, now Shaw Savill's *Ocean Monarch*, seen at Brisbane on the 30th July, 1970 before the conversion which proved so disastrous both for her owners and for the Cammell Laird shipyard. *Laurence Dunn collection.*

Ocean Monarch eventually emerged on the 17th September, twelve months after the work had begun. Her troubles were far from over, however. Her departure for Southampton was delayed when a dispute arose among members of her crew, who were complaining about conditions aboard. They alleged that the ventilation system was not working properly and walked off the ship. Nevertheless, after a meeting with the officers, they returned and *Ocean Monarch* sailed 90 minutes late. Sadly, it was just a foretaste of what was to come.

As in the conversion of *Empress of Britain* into *Queen Anna Maria*, a major area of the work had centred on the stern, replacing the tiered after decks with a large bar and dance floor, with an expansive lido deck above it. Overall, while *Ocean Monarch* retained most of her graceful appearance, this addition was not created with the same flair that had been given to the conversion of her sister. Thus, *Ocean Monarch* had a rather heavy look about her stern quarter: the small windows were totally different in style from any others along the sides of the ship and made the new structure so obviously an ill-conceived addition. Even internally, the room appeared to be poorly planned, built around the tank that contained the swimming pool on the deck above and with a badly sited dance floor. The brash orange and green colour scheme and the plastic furnishings were at odds with the gracious original décor

that remained in the rest of the public rooms. They would, in fact, have been more suited to a short sea ferry. However, this was a room designed to appeal to the essentially tourist class nature of the majority of Shaw Savill's passengers, whereas the restrained wood panelling and etched glass of the other areas reflected the ship's North Atlantic heritage and the fact that she had been designed over a decade earlier.

Apart from the new aft lounge, known as the Tavern, and the extensive lido deck, the refit had created over 130 new cabins, increasing the passenger capacity from 1,058 in two classes to 1,372 in one class. All of her aft cargo handling gear had been removed and cabins had been created in the spaces that had been taken up by the cargo hatch trunking. However, the largest group of new cabins was built down on D Deck, in spaces that had previously been used as cargo holds. Forward on A Deck, in space that had also been used for cargo purposes, more cabins were created.

Unfortunately, the delightful area that had once been the First Class Sun Deck and its Sun Lounge was also eliminated in order to provide space for another twenty-five cabins. Whereas in the conversion of the *Queen Anna Maria* most of the cabins were given private bathrooms, aboard *Ocean Monarch* many remained without this facility. This again was a reflection of the tourist class nature of her intended service, primarily out to Australia, as opposed to the trans-Atlantic service and the cruising rôle orientated to the American market, of her former sister. The conversion increased *Ocean Monarch*'s gross tonnage to 25,971.

She arrived in Southampton on the 19th September, 1971 and remained there for a month while finishing touches were made to her. She finally sailed on the 16th October, fully booked on the last of what should have been a full programme of summer cruises. Sadly, even this cruise did not get off to a good start, with the departure being delayed by health officials.

On the 5th November, she sailed from Southampton on what was to be the longest and most diverse voyage of her entire career: to Australia via the Panama Canal, California and the islands of the Pacific. Before passing through the Canal, she made stops at Acapulco, San Francisco (for two nights) and Vancouver. Then, it was out across the ocean to Honolulu and down to Suva before arriving in Auckland on the 17th December. *Ocean Monarch* arrived in Sydney on the 21st December but, strangely, no Christmas cruise had been planned for her

and she remained there until early January. She then made three cruises to New Zealand and the South Pacific islands of Fiji and Noumea before once again making another liner voyage back across the Pacific to Britain.

She arrived in Southampton on the 4th April, 1972 and on the 12th embarked passengers for perhaps the most ambitious of her voyages: seventy-four days around the World, sailing eastwards via Cape Town and Durban to Australia and returning via Tahiti, as she had on her previous homeward voyage. On the 8th July, she left Southampton on the initial sailing of a programme of seven Mediterranean cruises: her first for the British market except for the one that followed the fiasco of her refit. These were marketed as 'Sea Spectaculars' and her fleet-mate *Northern Star* also operated ten cruises as part of this series. Shaw Savill had announced the previous December that they were making some changes to the 1972 schedule they had planned for *Ocean Monarch*. Two 13-day cruises in September were to be replaced by one of 20 days. Passengers already booked on either of the 13-day cruises were to be offered the new 20-day one without additional charge – seven days of free cruising!

The remodelled *Ocean Monarch* made a few liner voyages to the Antipodes but was mainly a cruise ship. Throughout her career with Shaw Savill, she was beset by labour disputes. *Laurence Dunn collection.*

During the many months that *Ocean Monarch* had been stuck at the Cammell Laird yard, the face of long-haul trans-oceanic voyaging had begun to change. Already, Shaw Savill had withdrawn their much-loved liner *Southern Cross* from the Round-the-World service: from June, 1970, she had run purely as a cruise ship from Liverpool and had been earmarked for disposal once the newly refitted *Ocean Monarch* was fully operational. The enormous cost which would have been involved in changing her emigrant-style accommodation into something more acceptable to the demands of the modern cruise market forced the company to sell her and to concentrate their passenger operations on *Ocean Monarch* and *Northern Star*. Then, in November, 1970, Furness Withy, the parent company of Shaw Savill, made the shattering announcement that twenty-three of the ships owned by the companies in their group would be taken out of service, citing an unprecedented rate of escalation in operating expenses as the reason. The loss of so much income from all of *Ocean Monarch*'s cancelled cruises cannot have helped either. The three cargo/passenger liners *Akaroa*, *Aranda* and *Arawa* were amongst the vessels which were to be withdrawn by Shaw Savill and by the time *Ocean Monarch* had re-entered service they had left the fleet.

Other major operators for whom the passenger liner trade to Australia was a significant part of their business were also beginning to rationalise their fleets. In April, 1972, P&O withdrew the seventeen-year old *Iberia* from service and the *Orcades* followed her in October. Lauro Lines ceased their Australian service by December, 1972, placing their *Achille Lauro* and *Angelina Lauro* in full-time cruise service. Likewise, Sitmar Line had realised, once the Australian government had switched their lucrative migrant contract to the Chandris Line, that their future also lay in the cruise market rather than in line voyages between Europe and Australia. Chandris, of course, with that profitable contract and with the benefit of cheaper Greek crews, were able not only to continue offering a regular liner service but even added an additional ship, the 25,000-ton *Britanis*, to join their flagship *Australis* and the *Ellinis* on the route.

On the 3rd November, 1972, at the end of her first programme of 'Sea Spectaculars', *Ocean Monarch* sailed on another voyage to Australia and New Zealand via the Cape. It was to be her final such voyage for some considerable time as the Assisted Passage voyages for people emigrating to Australia were now solely in the hands of the Chandris Line. Shaw Savill therefore planned an exciting and far-reaching schedule of Pacific cruises for her that would last until April, 1974. Initially, it had been intended that she would make just two long cruises from Sydney along with her regular line voyages, but now the latter no longer appeared to be viable and, like every other passenger ship owner, Shaw Savill could see that the future lay in cruising. Thus, a programme of twenty-five cruises was drawn up, ranging in length from forty-six days to the occasional 'cruise to nowhere'.

This revised schedule was not appreciated by some of *Ocean Monarch*'s crew. Just as she was about to depart from Sydney on the 22nd January, 1973, over half her crew staged a mass walk-out over a pay dispute. They were claiming a $A35 per month bonus because the recent revaluation of the Australian dollar had seriously

Together with *Northern Star*, *Ocean Monarch* ran 'Sea Spectaculars', cruises from Southampton aimed particularly at the family market.
Luís Miguel Correia collection.

eroded the value of their wages, which were paid in sterling. This demand was met with a blank refusal and, instead, an offer of $A6 per month was made. The crew held a vote, with 191 refusing to accept the offer and electing instead to return to Britain. *Ocean Monarch* was eventually able to sail on the 25th with a much-reduced crew. About 700 of her original 900 passengers remained with the ship. The calls at Noumea and Pt. Vila had to be cancelled.

Replacement crew members were flown out to Australia to join the ship on her next cruise. In the meantime, some of her passengers helped out with onboard chores where possible. It was a sad fact that, for some reason, the unions never liked *Ocean Monarch*. There was often unrest and unruly behaviour aboard and it has often been said that she suffered acts of industrial sabotage. This bad attitude permeated the ship and as a result she would never enjoy the same happy atmosphere that had been very apparent on *Southern Cross* and that continued aboard *Northern Star*.

While most of her cruises were of approximately two weeks duration, with calls at the popular ports of Auckland, Suva, Lautoka and Noumea, several took her further afield to even more exotic locations. Between the 26th April and the 18th June, *Ocean Monarch* sailed to the Orient, with calls at Singapore, Hong Kong, Manila and Port Moresby. It was, however, the forty-six day trans-Pacific cruise that was perhaps her most exciting. She sailed from Sydney on the 22nd October, 1973, calling at Wellington and Auckland to embark further passengers before heading out into the South Pacific for Papeete, Tahiti. Then, it was onward to Los Angeles, San Francisco and Vancouver. On her way back to Auckland and Sydney, she made calls at Honolulu and Suva. The remaining cruises were of the more usual twelve to fourteen days duration. On the 1st May, 1974, *Ocean Monarch* once again set out across the Pacific, but this time it was on a line voyage back to Southampton.

On the 22nd June, she departed on a fifteen-day Mediterranean cruise, the first in another programme of 'Sea Spectaculars', which she again operated along with *Northern Star*. Although it was a difficult time for all shipowners, with continual increases in the price for bunkers which had to be reflected in supplements to the already announced fares, cruising from Southampton was enjoying quite a renaissance. Both *Ocean Monarch* and *Northern Star* had enjoyed considerable popularity, even against the likes of Union-Castle's *Reina del Mar*, the *Oriana* and *Canberra* of P&O and the Russian liners that were then operated by CTC Lines. However, their popularity was put to the test during the summer of 1974 as both Shaw Savill ships were troubled with mechanical breakdowns which received much coverage in the press and tarnished their image considerably. After one particularly serious breakdown in the Mediterranean, *Northern Star*'s passengers had to be flown back to Britain from Tunis. On the 14th September, shortly after having departed Southampton, *Ocean Monarch* suffered electrical defects as a result of generator trouble and had to return to port. The repairs took almost four days and she was only able to resume her cruise on the 18th.

On the 14th November, she boarded 800 passengers for another voyage out to Australia. This was also blighted by mechanical problems. As the ship crossed the Atlantic,

trouble with a boiler cut the production of fresh water, which had to be rationed. Repairs were made over the weekend of the 23rd and the 24th while she was in Barbados. However, the boiler was still troublesome as she made her way across the Caribbean and engineers were flown out to Panama to try to rectify the problem. Having disembarked her passengers in Sydney on the 20th December, *Ocean Monarch* went to Wooloomooloo for further repairs. Both her port and starboard main boilers and the port turbo-alternator rotor were in need of attention.

On the 8th January, 1975, she sailed on the first of her latest series of Pacific cruises, to Honiara, Lautoka and Suva. On her return to Sydney, she was again sent off to dry dock. Given that she had been experiencing severe engine problems, Shaw Savill had decided to cancel her next cruise and have their engineers give her a serious appraisal. It transpired that she required a large amount of work in her machinery spaces, work that would be both costly and time consuming to undertake.

On the 31st January, *Ocean Monarch* resumed her schedule of cruises. However, the fact that she was in need of a considerable amount of mechanical attention was somewhat underlined when further engine problems delayed her departure from Sydney on the 4th March for a 16-day cruise. Her passengers remained onboard, with a full programme of activities as though the cruise was progressing normally, although in fact the ship was still securely alongside the terminal while the repairs were made. At 11 pm on the 6th, she was finally able to sail. The company had already planned that this would be a rather shorter series of Sydney-based cruises, with the ship returning to the United Kingdom in June for a programme of what were being marketed as 'Shaw Savill Sea Quest Cruises', which she would run in conjunction with *Northern Star*. Even though *Ocean Monarch* had been sailing for Shaw Savill for five years, the company was still happy to trade off her past life: a fine photograph in the brochure was captioned '*Ocean Monarch* first made her name on the North Atlantic route to Canada: she is remembered with affection by many who sailed in her under the name *Empress of England*." It was unfortunate that Shaw Savill chose to recall those happier and rather more successful days at a time when her career was at this very lowest point.

Sadly, her planned series of cruises to the Mediterranean and the Atlantic islands was not to be. On the 1st April, it was announced that *Ocean Monarch* was to be withdrawn from service when she returned to the UK in June. In order to carry out the repairs she needed, her entire summer cruising season would have had to be cancelled. Given the loss of revenue this would entail, the high cost that the repairs would involve and the increased costs of operating passenger liners, Shaw Savill had decided to dispose of her. It was a blow to the company employees and to the cruising public, but worse was yet to come. A few weeks later, a further announcement was made: *Northern Star* would also be withdrawn, on the 1st November at the end of her cruising season. A Furness Withy spokesman explained that passenger ship operations were no longer viable as a result of inflated manning and bunkering costs. Cruise fares had been raised 30% and further increases would have been necessary if operations were to continue. Obviously, the fact that, like *Ocean*

Rust-streaked and troubled, *Ocean Monarch* is nearing the end of her career. By contrast, the other two 'Empresses' went on to enjoy a long period of brilliant success. *Luís Miguel Correia collection.*

Monarch, Northern Star was in need of considerable, and expensive, mechanical attention was an all-important factor in this decision.

The departure of the *Ocean Monarch* from Australia was marked by an unfortunate display of bad behaviour by her crew. She was due to sail on the 26th April but shortly before sailing time several crew members started throwing bottles, cans and other items from the ship, hitting people on the balcony of the Overseas Passenger Terminal who were there to wave farewell to the passengers. The police had to be called to restore order and the ship had to remain in port overnight. She sailed the following day, a humiliating end to an already less than successful chapter in her career.

During that final voyage back to Southampton, it was announced that she had been sold to Taiwanese ship breakers. *Ocean Monarch* arrived in Southampton on the 5th June, dressed overall and proudly flying a paying-off pennant. She berthed just astern of *Northern Star*, which had several months of cruising still ahead of her, which, ironically, were a huge success. She had over 1,000 passengers aboard for each trip. However, the decision had been made and *Northern Star* would ultimately follow

Ocean Monarch out to the breakers of Taiwan. *Ocean Monarch* remained in Southampton until the 13th June, being de-stored. Then, with all but two of her lifeboats removed, she made her stately progress down Southampton Water at the beginning of her final voyage. She passed Gibraltar on the 16th and was at Port Said on the 22nd. On the 10th July, she arrived off Singapore Roads and on the 17th she reached Kaohsiung, where she was to be broken up. Although her career had lasted just eighteen years and she was therefore the shortest-lived of the 'White Empresses', she was the most widely-travelled of them.

Speaking at the Furness Withy Group annual general meeting, Lord Beeching, the chairman since 1972, said: "Ships such as these inspire a strong sentimental attachment and I am sure that many of our shareholders will regret their passing, just as we do. Nevertheless, it must be said that from a financial point of view their disposal gives rise to nothing but a sigh of relief. They have become a loss-making worry and there could be no surer way of improving the profitability than by withdrawing them."

8

Mardi Gras

Empress of Canada was not destined to be idle in London's Tilbury Docks for very long. A ten-year old liner of such high quality and enviable reputation was bound to attract interest and it was hardly surprising that Home Lines, a company of quality and reputation itself, should be interested in the redundant 'Empress'. At the time, Home Lines were operating two ships out of New York on cruises to Bermuda and down to the Caribbean: the 1965-built 27,000-ton *Oceanic* and the 1931-built *Homeric*. Although a somewhat mismatched pair, they were both very successful and *Homeric*, despite her considerable vintage, was a much-loved ship with her own loyal following. However, she was certainly no match for the beautifully appointed *Oceanic* and Home Lines obviously felt that *Empress of Canada* would be the ideal ship to replace her. After all, she had already built up her own following during her regular winter sailings from New York. They even went as far as engaging consultants to prepare a detailed conversion proposal. Sadly, however, the project fell through.

Back in June, 1966, a Norwegian company, Klosters Sunward Ferries Ltd. had placed a new car/passenger ferry named *Sunward* on a cruise/ferry service out of Southampton to Vigo, Lisbon and Gibraltar. This strikingly designed ship hardly had time to make any real impression on the market, for after only a few months the border between Spain and Gibraltar was closed, thereby making the service redundant. Klosters were left with a brand new ship on their hands. At around the same time, two similar ferry/cruise ships, *Nili* and *Bilu*, owned by the Israeli company Somerfin, had been operating in the Caribbean. The Somerfin company, however, collapsed due to the failure of some of its European business interests and the operation of *Nili* and *Bilu* came to a sudden end. As the Israeli government was the mortgage-holder of the pair, they had them seized.

Mr. Ted Arison, an experienced Israeli engineer and the son of the former owner of one of the largest shipping firms in Israel, had served as the agent for the Caribbean operations of the Somerfin ships. He now found himself in

Empress of Canada in drydock at Tilbury in February, 1972 during her superficial conversion for the new Carnival Cruise Lines. An equally elegant Swedish Lloyd ferry lies nearby. *Laurence Dunn collection.*

the unfortunate position of having a sales and marketing organisation, along with a large number of booked passengers, but with no ships on which to accommodate them. However, a news article in *Travel Weekly* alerted Arison to the opposite problem being faced by the Klosters – a ship but no passengers. He contacted Klosters, suggesting that as *Sunward* was not unlike the Somerfin vessels that had proved to be very popular in the Caribbean market, it was probable that *Sunward* could generate similar popularity. Klosters grasped the opportunity, apparently stating: "Give us a guaranteed income of half a million dollars in the next year and you can have the agency for *Sunward*." At the time, Arison did not have the money but nevertheless made the guarantee. Within two weeks the Norwegian Caribbean Line had been set up and *Sunward* was moved across the Atlantic to operate 3- and 4-day cruises out of Miami, beginning on the 19th December, 1966.

For almost five years, all went well and Norwegian Caribbean Line prospered, adding three new ships to their fleet. But bad feeling had begun to develop between the Norwegians and the Arison team. There was disagreement over the terms of the ten year agency contract. In the summer of 1971, Knut Kloster served notice that Norwegian Caribbean intended to exercise an option allowing them to terminate it if certain financial targets were not met. Arison replied that profit figures had been sabotaged in order to provide an excuse to abort the contract and moved quickly to protect himself by seizing all advance money from the various NCL offices around America. He believed that the courts would decide that he was entitled to his commission. A subsequent lawsuit was settled out of court. Meanwhile, Klosters hired most of Arison's staff, leaving him with an organisation made up solely of senior executives and, once again, no ship! However, he was confident that he would soon be able to start up a cruise operation of his own and set his public relations team to work on an advertising campaign to promote the new operation. The slogan 'The Golden Fleet' was created but at the time it was little more than a golden dream.

At the time, there were two recently laid up liners that had generated considerable speculation regarding their futures: the Cunard vessels *Carmania* and *Franconia*. Although built in the mid-1950s as *Saxonia* and *Ivernia* for Cunard's Canadian services, they had been rebuilt with much more of a cruising capability in 1963 and had enjoyed considerable success for several years. However, by the late 1960s, Cunard were in a dire financial position and were faced with having to make radical cuts to their once large and prestigious fleet of Atlantic liners. *Carmania* and *Franconia*, in need of further expensive refits and modernisation, were just two of the casualties. Ted Arison felt that they could become the 'golden' ships of his fledgling cruise line and visited England to look over them. While his inspection confirmed that they were just what he wanted, it also revealed that they were not in as good condition as he had imagined. Cunard had hoped to sell them for £1,200,000 each. Given their condition, Arison followed the advice of the brokers and made an offer of a lower figure. In any case, he did not have sufficient resources to meet the asking price. Despite some negotiations, terms could not be agreed and the sale did not proceed.

Somewhat disheartened, he made plans to return to Miami. However, shortly before he was due to leave London, he was persuaded by a friend, Jacob Victor of the naval architects Technical Marine Planning, to visit the laid up *Empress of Canada* in Tilbury. It has been said that as he walked round her dimly-lit public rooms he fell in love with her and quickly realised her potential. Certainly, the more modern 'Empress' was much more promising than the Cunarders and would need less rebuilding and restyling to make her suitable as a Caribbean cruise ship. She would therefore be able to go into service in a relatively short time. Having failed to acquire *Carmania* and *Franconia*, Arison was determined not to let the superior *Empress of Britain* slip from his grasp. Thus, he turned to a friend whom he had known since his school days in Israel, Meshulam Riklis. Riklis was the chairman of a big conglomerate, Rapid American Corporation, and was also the main shareholder in American International

Travel Service Inc. (AITS) of Boston, which ran tours to various worldwide destinations, using the name Carnival.

AITS had already shown interest in expanding into the newly developing cruise industry. In 1969, they had acquired the former *Theodor Herzl*, a 10,000-ton liner that had belonged to Zim Israel Navigation Co., but which AITS registered under the ownership of New Horizons Shipping, Ltd. Although officially called *Carnivale*, she had the name *Carnival* painted on her bows. Plans were drawn up for her conversion into a cruise ship but, for some unexplained reason, they were not taken forward and AITS's intention to become part of the cruise industry was shelved for a short while. Arison suggested to Riklis that *Empress of Canada* would be the ideal vessel with which AITS could realise their aspirations. Riklis was persuaded to establish a subsidiary with the name Carnival Cruise Lines, to own and operate the ship and an agreement was reached for AITS to put forward $6.5 million to help finance the deal.

Ted Arison quickly began the arrangements for the purchase of *Empress of Canada*. The following weeks were a whirlwind of activity; everything was completed by January, 1972 and the ship was made ready for another trans-Atlantic voyage. On the 14th February, it was reported that she would be renamed *Mardi Gras* and would sail from Miami for the newly formed Carnival Cruise Lines. On the 21st, the former *Empress of Canada* officially became *Mardi Gras*.

She was due to sail for Miami that day but, yet again, members of the National Union of Seamen disrupted the plans. Sam McCluskie, the national organiser of the NUS, said: "We are picketing the ship in order to combat the growing menace of crews of convenience. Their low pay undermines the hard-won wages and conditions of seamen throughout the World." There were claims that concessionaires were to operate the ship's catering department at a wage of £18 per month. The union officials were able to persuade the tug crews and the Port of London Authority staff who operated the lock gates at Tilbury to 'black' the ship and pickets tried to get other seamen to join in the action. Initial talks between the International Transport Workers Federation, the National Union of Seamen and Carnival Cruise Lines failed to

reach an agreement. However, as *Mardi Gras* was due to sail on her first cruise from Miami on the 4th March and as this cruise was fully booked, any further delay would prove to be costly. On the 25th February, it was reported that after further discussions the NUS had settled its dispute with Carnival. The Union would not disclose the exact terms of the agreement but a spokesman said they had secured 'a substantial increase' in the rates of pay. On the 26th, *Mardi Gras* was eased out of Tilbury Docks into the fog-shrouded Thames. So began a career that was to reshape the cruise industry and make the former 'Empress' into a virtual cruising legend.

While Carnival Cruise Lines had got themselves a fine first ship, they were in fact financially very weak, so everything had to be done to contain costs. There was not even money for someone to design a smart new logo for the company: instead, they adapted the former Canadian Pacific funnel markings, changing the colours from shades of green and white to red, white and blue. But so that it did not look too similar to the CP logo, the angles were softened into curves. The broad green band around the hull was replaced by a narrower red one.

Given the precarious financial position of Carnival, it was essential that *Mardi Gras* should begin earning money immediately. However, her 4th March sailing had to be cancelled until a $1 million responsibility bond had been posted. There was no time for her to be refitted or to host receptions while she was alongside the dock in Miami. Just a minimum of superficial refurbishment work had been done prior to her departure from London, plus some other work during her voyage across the Atlantic. On the 11th March, 1972, a mere six weeks after her purchase, *Mardi Gras* departed Miami on her first cruise for Carnival Cruise Lines, with 300 members of the travel trade amongst her passengers.

Size matters: and it was important for the new company to promote the fact that their ship, at 25,780 gross tons, was the largest vessel sailing from Miami. Pride, however, comes before a fall. In those days, Miami's channel, Government Cut, was dredged to a depth of thirty feet. When *Mardi Gras* arrived from Tilbury she had entered the port, light. However, by the time she was ready to sail on her maiden voyage for Carnival, her draught at

An early Carnival Cruise Lines postcard. The reverse bears the inscriptions 'The Golden Fleet' and 'AITS… the people who give you the world'. *Author's collection.*

the stern was twenty-nine feet six inches. Although, on the recommendation of the pilot, she was re-trimmed and her master waited until the flood tide, a stiff northeast gale turned her bow as she passed beyond the breakwater at the harbour entrance. A misunderstood, or inaccurate, rudder command from the pilot to the helmsman resulted in a sharp turn to starboard instead of to port and, as a consequence, *Mardi Gras* grounded gently but firmly on the limestone and coral bottom south of Government Cut.

There followed a day of unsuccessful attempts to get the ship afloat and into deep water. Carnival staff, positioned on the stone breakwater communicated with Arison and the ship's captain via 'walkie-talkies', in Hebrew to maintain secrecy. But the fact that *Mardi Gras* was aground and that attempts were being made to refloat her was obvious for all to see. Eventually, after more than 24 hours of fruitless effort, it was decided that the tugs should all be positioned so that they could take the passengers off the ship: the cruise would have to be abandoned. With everyone so thoroughly downhearted and with the image of Ted Arison's 'Golden Fleet' looking rather tarnished, *Mardi Gras*' captain decided to have the tugs try one more time to refloat her – and it worked. *Mardi Gras* was at last free.

Divers were sent down to inspect the hull and they discovered that, very fortunately, she had been stuck directly beneath the keel, where the plating and framing were strongest. Most importantly, she was not taking in water. However, visual conditions were poor and the divers had only been able to ascertain that the hull was dented but seemingly otherwise undamaged. The cruise could continue. It was a most inauspicious beginning but the media attention certainly made people aware of *Mardi Gras*. As it tuned out, there was considerable damage to the hull plating and about 75% of her underwater area had to be replaced in a subsequent refit. With Ted Arison's less than amicable departure from Norwegian Caribbean Line, Klosters were watching the development of his new company closely. Aware that Carnival Cruise Lines could possibly become a serious competitor, they viewed the grounding with some amusement and a cocktail called 'Mardi Gras On The Rocks' was created for sale aboard their ships.

Mardi Gras had commenced her new career virtually as

Canadian Pacific had left her, with only essential maintenance work having been done. In those early days, she was in many respects still essentially *Empress of Canada*. Gradually, during her initial cruises, different areas of the ship were refurbished, with parts of her accommodation being sectioned off while the work was in progress. With the company still in a precarious financial position, there was no real opportunity to do more than superficial redecoration to the public rooms. Carnival were quite simply unable to afford to take *Mardi Gras* out of service, have her dry-docked and transform her into the cruise ship they wanted. The company had an operations staff of just twelve people, who did the crewing, the technical work and the arrangements for passenger service and for the entertainment.

With the ship remaining in service, her two-in-a-cabin passenger capacity was increased from 808 to 906 and those cabins without private facilities were rebuilt to include both shower and toilet. As each area was refurbished, the wooden panelled walls would often be covered with vibrantly coloured metal foil wallpaper in an attempt to generate the more relaxed and casual atmosphere that Carnival were striving for. The public rooms were renamed and put to new uses: the former First Class Mayfair Room became the Showboat Club casino. The St. Lawrence Club was now the Showboat Lounge and the Windsor Lounge became the Carousel Lounge and bar, while the Banff Club was transformed into the Point After Club discotheque.

Initially, both restaurants were used but because it was known that the forward one had originally been reserved for First Class passengers, this caused resentment among some people aboard the now one-class vessel. Sadly, therefore, this most handsome room was soon demolished and in its place more cabins were created. The indoor pool was retained, still with its original clever name Coral Pool. As *Mardi Gras* was now purely a cruise ship, she no longer had any need for her cargo-handling equipment and most of her derricks and booms were removed, with the exception of the two forward ones. This undoubtedly enhanced her appearance considerably and was done during a 50-day dry-docking which finally took place after she had been in service for some while. Canadian Pacific had let it be known that they were unhappy with Carnival's somewhat blatant hi-jacking of their company logo and requested that it be further modified. In fact, this worked in Carnival's favour since the after blue area of the funnel was extended, reducing in thickness the white section. The new design even more echoed the 'C' of Carnival – albeit backwards!

Despite the promotion of *Mardi Gras* as an informal fun cruise ship, she was also still being marketed as 'the flagship of the Golden Fleet'. Given that Carnival Cruise Line was a single ship operation, this was somewhat pretentious. Nevertheless, the casual, fun image was attractive to many who had previously seen cruises as being stuffy, formal and only for the elderly. The new image generated good passenger loads for *Mardi Gras*. Nevertheless, for two years Carnival appeared to be just one step away from bankruptcy. A story that Ted Arison himself would often tell to illustrate the difficult times the company went through was that on one occasion, when attempting to get the ship refuelled in San Juan, he found that the fuel suppliers would only accept payment in cash. He had no choice but to go round emptying all the cash registers in the casinos, bars and shops in order to ensure that the ship had sufficient fuel to get back to Miami!

By 1974, AITS had begun to lose interest in Carnival Cruise Lines. The previous year, they had bought an hotel in Las Vegas and the Nevada Gaming Commission had already indicated that they wanted them to divest themselves of their interest in the cruise business. The rapidly increasing costs of operating the ship due to the rise in oil prices and the fact that, despite *Mardi Gras'* healthy passenger loads, the company still had $5 million of debts must all have contributed further to their disenchantment. Ted Arison, however, still had utmost confidence in the venture but he could see that *Mardi Gras* and Carnival could not realise their full potential as a purely single-ship operation. But as Carnival appeared

to be continually flirting with bankruptcy, there was no suitable ship on the second-hand market that they could consider purchasing.

So Arison tried a different approach: a joint operation with some other shipping line. Aware that the Greek Line were having difficulties, he approached the Goulandris family to see whether they would consider running *Queen Anna Maria* in tandem with *Mardi Gras*, even offering them a half-interest in Carnival. In a misguided business decision, Arison's proposal was turned down. (It is interesting to speculate whether, if Basil Goulandris had been alive, he would have accepted the joint venture and Greek Line would still have existed to-day, albeit as part of the Carnival empire.) With Greek Line's refusal, an approach was made to another Greek operator, Sun Line, who also turned the idea down.

In its final days, the German Atlantic Line had operated cruises in the Pacific with their ship *Hamburg*, in

Umbrellas, awnings and loungers: *Mardi Gras* **was not only the largest cruise ship sailing out of Miami, but also emphatically a 'Fun Ship'.** *Author's collection.*

conjunction with Holland America's *Statendam*. Following the demise of German Atlantic, Arison had his team explore in some depth the possibility of a similar operational agreement between *Statendam* and *Mardi Gras*. However, like the other lines, Holland America had no time for any form of alliance with the fledgling and obviously fragile Carnival Cruise Lines. No one wished to be associated with a company that appeared to be on the verge of bankruptcy.

With AITS under pressure to cease their involvement with Carnival, an agreement was made for it to sell the loss-making line and its $5 million of debts to Ted Arison for a token payment of one dollar. In November, 1974, a new holding company was formed, the Carnival Corporation.

Ted Arison drew upon his years of ship-operating experience. Now free of the burden of other decision-makers, he could focus upon what needed to be done and how he could enable *Mardi Gras* to realise the potential that he had seen in her in that quiet wintry Tilbury backwater. Immediately, he began to reshape the entire operation of the ship. To the surprise of the cruise industry at large, within just one month *Mardi Gras* managed at last to turn a voyage profit. Changes aboard continued: the ship was altogether livened up. There was more music, more gambling opportunities, more fun, with the focus on activities for the 25 to 40 age group. *Mardi Gras* still had on board the same orchestra that had been there when she was *Empress of Canada*. They recalled the fact that she had generally been a very happy ship, for both crew and passengers, and out of this the 'Fun Ship' concept was born and the image of 'the flagship of the Golden Fleet' was dropped.

That *Mardi Gras* should have proved to be so popular from the very outset was remarkable. While Canadian Pacific had designed her with a cruising rôle in mind, she nevertheless still presented a very traditional ocean liner profile; and despite the superficial redecorations with vivid metallic wall coverings, she was also still very traditional internally. Although the seven-day circuit on which she was employed out of Miami to Nassau, San Juan and St. Thomas was highly lucrative, she had to meet the competition of the new, purpose-built ships of the Royal Caribbean Cruise Line and, of course, Norwegian Caribbean Line. These new ships were complete with well-designed and sheltered lido decks – as opposed to a tank dropped into a redundant cargo hatch on the *Mardi Gras* – and they also had vibrant modern public rooms with expansive windows to allow the bright Caribbean sunlight to flood in. Aboard *Mardi Gras*, the public rooms were inboard of a traditional enclosed promenade deck, all designed to cocoon her passengers from the turbulent North Atlantic.

However, with their strong emphasis on 'fun', Carnival had found the winning formula. In 1975, *Mardi Gras* was rated as being the Number One 7-day cruise ship sailing the Caribbean. Her reputation as a truly 'Fun Ship' was vigorously promoted, not only by travel agents but by her passengers as well, so that she became the most popular and best-liked ship sailing from Miami. In order to maintain this winning formula, Ted Arison knew that he had to find *Mardi Gras* a running mate.

After struggling at first to stave off bankruptcy, Carnival Cruise Lines quickly became an amazing success despite having only one ship, *Mardi Gras*, seen here at Nassau. *Luís Miguel Correia collection.*

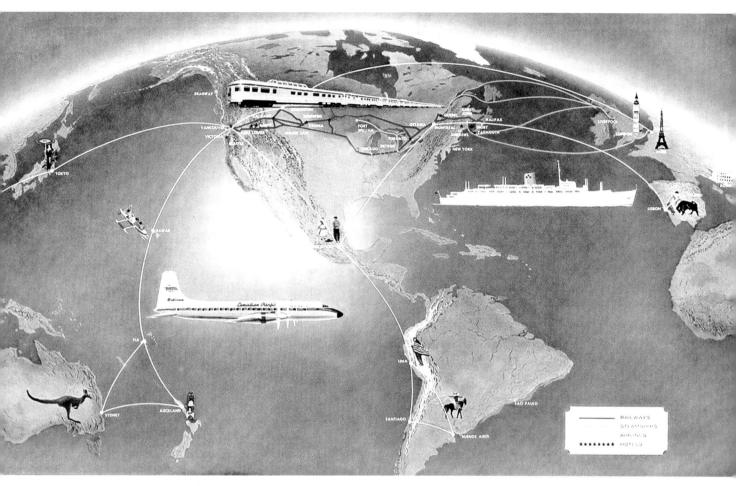

The almost worldwide reach of the Canadian Pacific network. *Author's collection.*

'For fun on the way': this Canadian Pacific advertisement foreshadows the 'Fun Ship' concept of Carnival Cruise Lines, the later owners of two of the 'White Empresses'. In fact, there was a world of difference between the rather formal Canadian Pacific style of the 'fifties and 'sixties and the hectic atmosphere of the Carnival ships. *Author's collection.*

When *Empress of Britain* came out in 1956, the First Class Sun Lounge and Drawing Room were, to British and Canadian eyes, very modern. *Author's collection.*

An artist's rendering of *Empress of Britain*'s Empress Room, where First and Tourist Class passengers could 'meet on neutral ground' and which 'accents the streamlined beauty of this new ship'. *Author's collection.*

Empress of England in the new green and white livery which, in many people's opinion, did little for the appearance of the handsome 'Empress' liners. *Author's collection.*

A postcard view of the autumnal coloured Thames Dining Room on *Empress of England*.
Author's collection.

This forward-facing, crescent-shaped room on *Empress of England* was known as the Garden Lounge – although the vegetation was somewhat sparse.
Author's collection.

The Banff Club cocktail lounge on *Empress of Canada* illustrated the current fashion of providing Tourist Class passengers with public rooms which were almost as luxurious as those in First Class.
Author's collection.

The name of the stylish Salle Frontenac, *Empress of Canada*'s First Class restaurant, was a reminder that the 'Empresses' sailed into the French-speaking ports of Québec and Montreal. *Author's collection.*

The First Class St. Lawrence Club on *Empress of Canada*. Some of its handsome décor survived throughout the ship's long career. *Author's collection.*

Very much in the 'sixties style, the dramatically coloured Windsor Lounge was a pleasant room for *Empress of Canada*'s Tourist Class passengers. *Author's collection.*

'*Empress of Canada.* Ultimate travel luxury. Air conditioned throughout, stabilized to take you from Liverpool to Montreal in six high-life days of relaxed, indulgent comfort.'
Author's collection.

Canadian Pacific had been well-known for their cruises out of New York since pre-War days. As the 'sixties progressed, cruising became steadily more important to the survival of their liners. *Author's collection.*

Models and, perhaps, some real passengers relax on the enclosed promenade of *Empress of Canada* – one of the traditional pleasures of a sea voyage. *Author's collection.*

Unlike some of their contemporaries, the post-War Canadian Pacific liners were designed to be easily adaptable for cruising. *Author's collection.*

Cruise the
caribbean

EMPRESS
OF CANADA
FROM
NEW YORK

CP
Ships

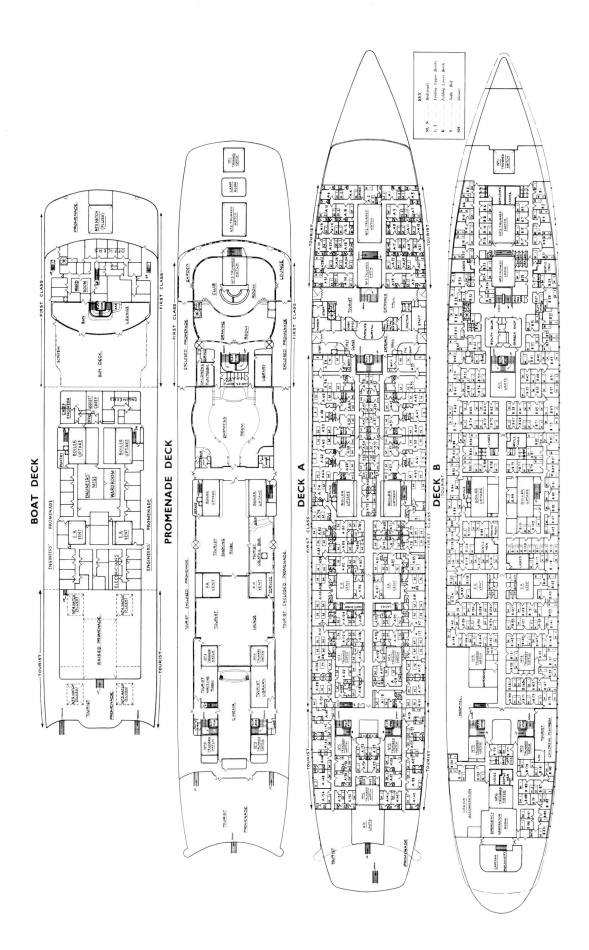

Plans of some of the *Empress of Britain*'s decks. The Boat Deck and Promenade Deck contained most of the public rooms. *Author's collection.*

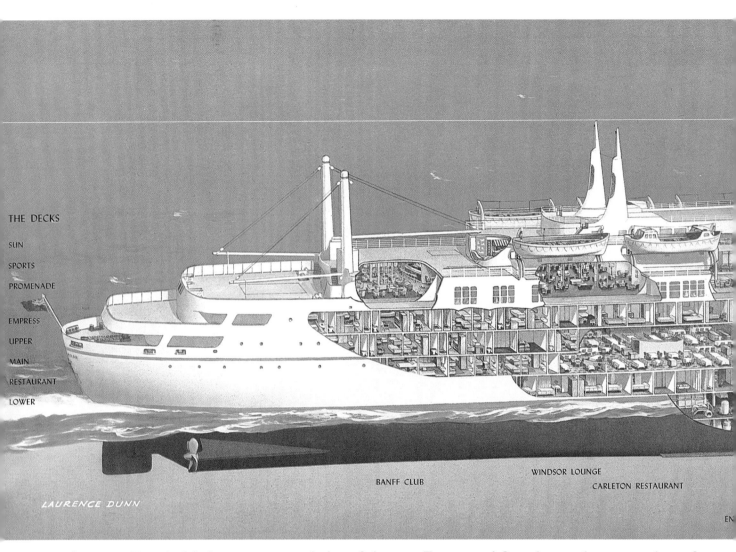

THE DECKS

SUN

SPORTS

PROMENADE

EMPRESS

UPPER

MAIN

RESTAURANT

LOWER

LAURENCE DUNN

BANFF CLUB

WINDSOR LOUNGE

CARLETON RESTAURANT

EN

Laurence Dunn's fabulous cut-away painting of the new *Empress of Canada* was the centre-piece of an introductory brochure. *Author's collection.*

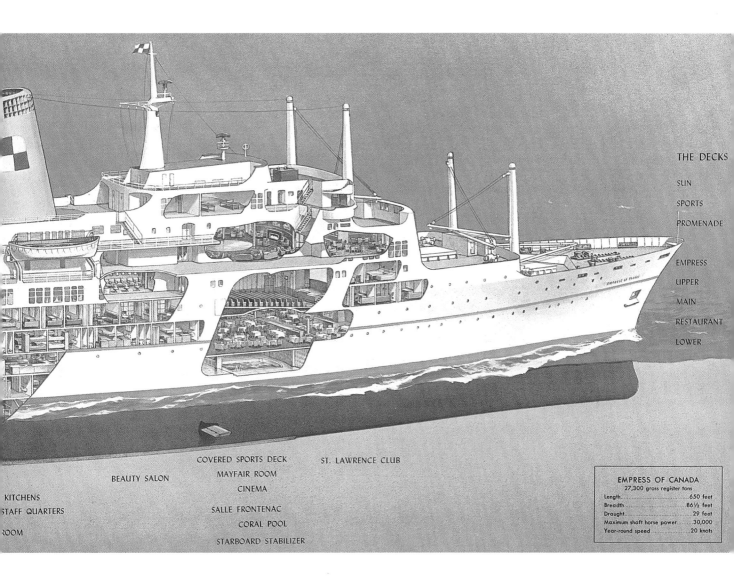

THE DECKS

SUN

SPORTS

PROMENADE

EMPRESS

UPPER

MAIN

RESTAURANT

LOWER

COVERED SPORTS DECK   ST. LAWRENCE CLUB

BEAUTY SALON   MAYFAIR ROOM

CINEMA

KITCHENS

STAFF QUARTERS   SALLE FRONTENAC

CORAL POOL

ROOM

STARBOARD STABILIZER

EMPRESS OF CANADA	
27,300 gross register tons	
Length	650 feet
Breadth	86½ feet
Draught	29 feet
Maximum shaft horse power	30,000
Year-round speed	20 knots

Canadian Pacific

Ocean Monarch

26,000 tons of wonderful life at sea

Shaw Savill Line

When *Empress of England* went to the Shaw Savill Line, she became their Tourist Class-only ship *Ocean Monarch*, on which 'you have the right to enjoy all the amenities, all the public rooms, all the service.' *Luis Miguel Correia collection.*

Ocean Monarch was very well provided with open deck space and had both a heated outdoor pool and a smaller indoor pool. *Author's collection.*

Ocean Monarch at Southampton. Her funnel has been painted in Shaw Savill's own particular shade of buff.
Luís Miguel Correia collection.

Ocean Monarch's Tavern, with its 50 ft.-long bar and dance floor, looked out over the stern.
Author's collection.

The built-up stern given to *Ocean Monarch* during her conversion was less felicitously designed than that of *Queen Anna Maria*. *Luis Miguel Correia.*

A bow view of *Mardi Gras* in her early days with Carnival. Just visible on the left is one of the ships of the Norwegian Caribbean Line, Carnival's great rival. *Author's collection.*

The Grand Ballroom on *Mardi Gras* looks positively restrained in comparison with the phantasmagorical interiors of the present-day Carnival ships. *Author's collection.*

The Mardi Gras nightclub during *Carnivale*'s early days. Behind the bandstand is some of the metallic wallpaper with which Carnival Cruise Lines sought to give the restrained Canadian Pacific décor a brighter touch. *Author's collection.*

Carnivale's 250-seat Riverboat Lounge had a bar, of course, but also some of the slot machines so important to the economics of cruise ship operation. *Author's collection.*

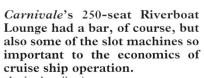

In her final Royal Olympic days, with a blue hull and gold sheer line, *Apollon* looked better than at almost any time in her long career. Here she is departing Heraklion. *J. D. Elliott.*

The distinctive funnel of *The Topaz* during the early days of the Thomson charter. Later the coloured bands became broader. *Author.*

The Topaz **at Kusadasi in later Thomson Cruises colours. After a troubled start, she became extremely well-liked by Thomson's passengers.** *Author.*

A crew member's tribute to his ship, painted on a quayside wall at Funchal in 2003. The flags presumably represent the nationalities of her crew. *Anthony Cooke.*

For the first time in over fifty years, an 'Empress' is seen in Vancouver. *Topaz* now wears Peace Boat livery. *Peter Knego.*

Although the Peace Boat organisation have made little change to *Topaz*'s interiors, they have been adapted for their purposes. *Peter Knego.*

Nearing the end: *Apollon* laid up at Eleusis in November, 2003. Behind her lies *Stella Solaris*. Both ships would soon make the sad last voyage to be broken up. *Peter Knego.*

Still looking stylish, *Apollon* waits to be dragged up the beach at Alang in India, where she will be scrapped. *Kaushal B. Trivedi. Copyright P.K. Productions, 2004.*

9

Carnivale

Following her ignominious departure from New York, *Queen Anna Maria* arrived in Piraeus on the 22nd January, 1975 and, shortly afterwards was placed in lay up at Perama along with many other redundant liners, including her fleetmate *Olympia*. Unlike *Olympia*, *Queen Anna Maria* was destined for only a brief stay in this forlorn bay of rusting and neglected vessels. After Greek Line went into receivership, the Chase Manhattan Bank, holders of the mortgages on both ships, were anxious to dispose of them and made them available for sale at a very low price.

Ted Arison had the two ships inspected. *Olympia*, having more recently been refitted, was in better condition and was cleaner. On the other hand, *Queen Anna Maria* had far greater potential as a cruise ship. However, Arison was not the only one who saw possibilities in her. Sitmar Line had enjoyed considerable success with their cruise ships *Fairwind* and *Fairsea*, the converted Cunarders *Carinthia* and *Sylvania* (which had been the direct competitors to the Canadian Pacific 'Empresses' on the St. Lawrence service). Sitmar too were looking to expand their operations with the acquisition of another vessel. When the Carnival inspection party arrived on board *Queen Anna Maria*, they found that her turbine covers had already been removed: representatives of the Sitmar Line had recently looked her over. Although all the correct procedures had initially been followed in her laying up, she had been left in the care of just one or two people and by the time Carnival's team came along, the ship was in a filthy state.

Having already seen that she would make an ideal running-mate for *Mardi Gras* (after all, they were near-sisters), Ted Arison once again entered into negotiations to acquire the ship: but, this time, he would buy her, the purchase price being just $3 million. So, in the end, the refusal by Greek Line to enter into a joint operation with Carnival turned out to Arison's benefit: he got their flagship after all, and at a bargain price!

Carnival's purchase of *Queen Anna Maria* was completed in December, 1975 and it was announced that she would be renamed *Carnivale*. As with the acquisition of *Mardi Gras*, things moved fast. Without shipyard work, she was made ready to cross the Atlantic once again, to Miami. She arrived there on New Year's Day, 1976. She was then sent to the Newport News shipyard in Virginia for dry-docking, cleaning and general repairs and for the adoption of Carnival's distinctive red, white and blue livery. By February, barely six weeks after her purchase, *Carnivale* was ready to enter her new owners' service. There had been time to replace carpeting and to do some other basic work but that was all; and, as a result, plumbing problems were extensive at first. Despite a less than perfect first cruise, the general reaction of the travel trade was positive. After a separation of twelve years, the two remaining 'Empresses' were together again and under circumstances that no one could ever have imagined when they were the pride of the Canadian Pacific fleet.

The former *Queen Anna Maria*, now called *Carnivale*, made an ideal running-mate for *Mardi Gras* and soon matched her in popularity. *Luís Miguel Correia.*

At the request of Canadian Pacific, Carnival Cruise Lines changed their funnel logo. The white crescent was now much thinner. *Luis Miguel Correia.*

It took Carnival about a year really to get *Carnivale* back into good shape, such had been the lack of care and maintenance during her final days with Greek Line. It was therefore encouraging that during that first year of operation she achieved an average load factor of 95 per cent. *Mardi Gras* had attracted passenger loads in excess of 100 per cent during the previous year. Of the two ships, *Carnivale* was the better suited to a cruising rôle, given the extensive rebuilding that Greek Line had given her, particularly in the creation of her large and novel lido deck.

Although in their 1976 brochure, Carnival promoted her with the line: 'discover a new world on the *Carnivale*', there was in fact nothing new about her itinerary. She too was based in Miami and ran on a seven-day circuit to San Juan, St, Maarten and St. Thomas. This was, however, a very popular route and her passengers were aboard as much for the ship's high spirited atmosphere as for the ports of call. With her entry into their service, Carnival were able to promote their 'Fun Ship' experience more fully – an experience that ensured that both the former 'Empresses' sailed from Miami full, week in, week out.

During those first months of service, *Carnivale* underwent marginal upgrading and refitting. The First Class Drawing Room and Cocktail Bar were opened up to make one large room: the Fly-Aweigh Discotheque. The former Empress Room, more latterly the Olympian Ballroom, became the Mardi Gras Nightclub. The original Tourist Class Smoking Room was renamed Riverboat Lounge, while the Tourist Class Lounge was refitted as the Riverboat Club Casino. Reading and writing rooms were turned into shops and what had once been a small chapel became the children's playroom. As on the *Mardi Gras*, the former First Class Dining Room was removed and cabins were built into the space. Once again, the decorative changes were superficial, with more of the metallic wallpaper covering the staid 'ocean liner style' panelling in an effort to project a more modern and light-hearted image. Gradually, some of the heavy, ponderous North Atlantic furnishings were replaced by lighter, bright, metal-frame furniture, some of which seemed oddly out of place in a ship that still exuded an air of quiet, gracious elegance.

Although *Carnivale* was still a trans-Atlantic liner at heart, her introduction marked the turning point for the company. While *Mardi Gras* had attracted large numbers of passengers virtually from the moment she entered Carnival's service, there was something about *Carnivale* that made her an even greater success – a certain atmosphere, an indefinable spirit that ensured she was the more popular of the two ships. The demand for cruises aboard the 'Fun Ships' was so great that in her first year of operation *Carnivale* set an occupancy record. The demand for *Mardi Gras*, too, continued unabated. In 1976, the two ships ran at an overall occupancy rate in excess of 100%; and 1977 saw both achieving a combined occupancy rate of 106.3%. (100% occupancy is based on two persons to a cabin and many cabins aboard *Mardi Gras* and *Carnivale* had upper berths to accommodate a third or fourth person.)

Even though, in those early days, they were essentially Miami-based ships, the pair occasionally operated cruises from other ports. For example, on the 16th September, 1975, *Mardi Gras* embarked 940 passengers at Baltimore for a Caribbean cruise. This was the largest number yet carried from the Maryland port by a cruise ship. During 1977, the two ships ran some cruises out of Norfolk, Virginia: *Carnivale* made four to Bermuda and the Caribbean, while *Mardi Gras* undertook a single voyage to Bermuda and back.

From being a company that every cruise industry watcher had expected to topple into bankruptcy at any moment, Carnival had emerged triumphant. The popularity of the two ships continued to grow. 'Carnival's got the fun' was the advertising slogan and it ensured that the ships sailed at remarkable levels of occupancy every week. Although both had enjoyed some measure of success with Canadian Pacific, this had been rather short-lived due to the changing patterns of travel. But under the guiding hand of Ted Arison and his team, the two 'Empresses' achieved undreamed-of success and within a very short time they had paid for themselves. Already, Ted Arison was beginning to look around for yet another ship upon which to work his winning 'Fun Ship' formula.

10

Carnival's got the Fun, and the Ships!

Another victim of the great changes in the world of passenger shipping during the 1970s was the joint service operated by Union-Castle Line and Safmarine between the United Kingdom and South Africa. The demise of this service was brought about not just because of the dominance of the airlines, nor because of the increases in the cost of oil – though obviously these were contributing factors. The primary reason was cargo containerisation. The liners employed by Union-Castle and Safmarine had vast cargo holds and it was the carriage of cargo, rather more than of passengers, which had ensured their viability. In 1974, five liners were still employed on the service but by 1976 the number had been reduced to just three: *Pendennis Castle*, *Windsor Castle* and *S.A.Vaal* (formerly the *Transvaal Castle*). The withdrawals continued and on her arrival in Southampton on the 14th June, 1976, the eighteen-year old *Pendennis Castle* – which, coincidentally, was known as the 'Fun Ship' of the fleet – was taken out of service. Five months later, on the 15th November, the announcement was made that the two remaining passenger mail ships were to be withdrawn in the latter part of 1977.

In the Spring of 1977, it was announced that *S.A.Vaal* had been sold to the Festivale Maritime Corporation of Panama: this company was, in fact, a subsidiary of Carnival Cruise Lines. Ted Arison, having been alerted to the fact that these two potentially useful liners were soon to come onto the market, had asked his assistant Meshulam Zonis to make an inspection of *S.A.Vaal*. Zonis was captivated by the possibilities offered by the ship, though at first glance she appeared an unlikely candidate for conversion into a cruise ship. Part of her attraction was that, unlike the two former 'Empresses', *S.A.Vaal* had a

relatively small passenger area, as well as large cargo holds. She therefore offered Carnival an almost blank canvas upon which virtually to design a new cruise ship to their own specifications. For the first time, they could afford to do this.

Often, they had looked at both *Mardi Gras* and *Carnivale*, trying to work out how they might add more cabins. Zonis realised that *S.A.Vaal* offered Carnival unlimited space in which to do what they wanted. On his advice, Arison moved quickly, for while he knew that he had found his third ship, there were other potential buyers expressing serious intent, amongst them once again the Sitmar Line. Arison, however, had a friendly relationship with Sitmar and he knew that they were also looking at the *Windsor Castle*, which, indeed, he had also expressed interest in acquiring. He went ahead and authorised the purchase of *S.A.Vaal* without having looked at the ship himself. When the broker called, asking permission to sell *Windsor Castle*, he agreed, thinking that he would be able to come to some agreement with Sitmar later on. However, much to his annoyance, he soon discovered that it was the Greek oil and shipping entrepreneur John Latsis, and not Sitmar Line, that had bought the ship. Thus, this handsome liner was lost to the World as an active passenger vessel and would spend many years in a curious limbo as an accommodation vessel, with even longer periods in lay-up.

On Saturday, the 29th October, 1977, with her funnel repainted grey and with the new name *Festivale* on her bows, this latest addition to the Carnival fleet departed Southampton. She was heading east to Japan, rather than to the Caribbean. As a result of an international tender, Kawasaki Heavy Industries had obtained the order for the

Not much more than a year after their purchase of *Carnivale*, Carnival Cruise Lines added the 38,000-ton *Festivale*, the former *Transvaal Castle* and *S.A. Vaal*, to their fleet. *Author.*

As *Mardi Gras'* passenger spaces were gradually altered, her character changed. The restrained Mayfair Room became the Showboat Club casino. *Author.*

$20 million conversion of the passenger/cargo liner into an all-passenger cruise ship. The contract called for Kawasaki to complete the conversion at its Kobe works between May and August. With a much-expanded superstructure containing a whole array of new public rooms and lido areas, *Festivale* emerged from the rebuilding able to accommodate 1,433 passengers in 580 cabins, as opposed to her former 725 in 353 cabins. The crew capacity had been increased from 415 to 579.

Festivale joined *Mardi Gras* and *Carnivale* in October, 1978 and as a consequence there was a rearrangement of itineraries. All three ships were still based in Miami (though Carnival had been giving some consideration to placing either *Mardi Gras* or *Carnivale* on cruises from New York). *Festivale* departed on Saturdays for San Juan, St. Thomas and St. Maarten, while *Mardi Gras* and *Carnivale* sailed on Sundays at 4 pm with the Dominican Republic as their new destination. *Carnivale* called at Samana, located on the northeastern coast of the island, before continuing to San Juan and then to St. Croix in the U.S. Virgin Islands. *Mardi Gras* meanwhile sailed for the capital of the Dominican Republic, Santo Domingo, then to St. Thomas and Nassau.

However, in August, 1979, *Mardi Gras* was sent on a cruise northwards to Canada. She arrived in Montreal on the 28th, receiving a fireboat welcome – it was her first visit to the port in eight years. In his address to the crowd that had gathered to welcome the liner, Mayor Jean Drapeau waxed nostalgic, stating that the "respectable lady of the sea has been transformed from a dowager into a debutante." Carnival had promoted the nine-day Boston to Montreal cruise as a 'homecoming'. It was a term that meant different things to different people. For the company and for the mayor, it meant the return of the ship to its former terminal port; but for many passengers – New Englanders with Canadian origins – it was a return to the land of their roots. Carnival invited over 700 guests to the ship for the welcoming ceremonies and cocktail parties. *Mardi Gras* departed at midnight, calling at Quebec on her way back to Boston. Mayor Drapeau had been happy to welcome the ship back to Montreal and was delighted with the announcement that Carnival planned a similar cruise for the following year. It seemed as though perhaps Montreal would be able to resume its long association with the 'Empress' ships. Indeed, *Mardi Gras* did return in August, 1980. She operated a 5-day cruise from Montreal to Boston, Charlottetown and Saguenay; and then a 4-day cruise to Quebec, which ended in Boston. That, however, was it and the former *Empress of Canada* never returned to the St. Lawrence.

Amongst the few initial changes which Carnival made when they placed *Carnivale* in Caribbean cruise service had been the renaming of some of her decks, following the pattern established by *Mardi Gras*. Thus, what had been Upper Deck had become Empress Deck while Main, Restaurant and 'A' Decks were now Upper, Main and Riviera Decks, respectively. This same pattern of naming continued with *Festivale*, so that she too acquired an Empress Deck. This pleasing tradition, obviously born of practicality and simplification throughout the fleet, continued long after Carnival disposed of the two former 'Empresses' and, by default, kept alive that little bit of Canadian Pacific tradition. At the same time, Carnival also helped in keeping alive some of the spirit of the major Italian shipping companies. As Carnival was emerging as a dominant name in the cruise market, the traditional state-funded Italian liner companies were being wound down. Carnival was therefore able to recruit very experienced Italian officers, both in the deck and engineering departments, which helped infuse the ships with that additional flair and continental atmosphere.

In 1972, when *Mardi Gras* had entered service for Carnival Cruise Lines, they were able to promote her as being the largest ship sailing out of Miami. With the introduction of *Festivale*, 38,175 gross tons, they could still lay claim to that distinction; and in their publicity material they were also anxious to promote the fact that she was the sixth largest passenger ship in the World. Ahead of her were *Queen Elizabeth 2* at 67,139 gross tons; *France* at 66,348 – but she was inactive at that time – *Canberra* at 44,807; *Oriana* at 41,920; and the 38,664-ton *Rotterdam*.

However, a challenge was beginning to take shape over the horizon, on the other side of the Atlantic. The executives at Carnival's arch rivals, Norwegian Caribbean Line, had watched with surprised fascination as Arison's once-fragile company had gone from strength to strength. His purchase and conversion of the redundant *S.A. Vaal* had been viewed as nothing short of foolhardy. Yet, like her fleetmates *Mardi Gras* and *Carnivale*, she had been an instant hit with the cruising public. In June, 1979, Knut Utstein Kloster, chairman of Klosters Rederi A/S, parent of NCL, bought the laid-up Atlantic liner *France*. His plan was to have her totally rebuilt as a Miami-based cruise ship, offering NCL's own brand of 'fun ship' cruising. Renamed *Norway*, she re-entered service in June, 1980. By this time, the port of Miami was acknowledged to be the Cruise Capital of the World, with many thousands of people departing on a whole variety of ships each week. In order to help cope with the continued growth in the number of passengers, Royal Caribbean Cruise Line (RCCL) had already had one of their vessels lengthened. Now, at the time of *Norway*'s entry into service, work was completed on the stretching of a second RCCL ship. In 1982, they would take delivery of a new and much larger vessel.

Ted Arison, Carnival Cruise Lines and their three

Décor on the Carnival ships became more extravagant as time went on. On *Carnivale*, the big night club at the stern was refurnished in a heavily patterned style. *Peter Knego.*

This enclosed promenade on *Carnivale* was given a marble floor and metallic ceilings in a 'make-over' by Joe Farcus. *Author.*

former British liners had been instrumental in changing the whole nature of cruising and the public's perception of it. In fact, Arison, as much as any other single person, could take the credit for the development of the modern cruise industry. Although there were several companies operating year-round out of Miami, including Royal Caribbean, it was Carnival and Norwegian Caribbean Line that always appeared to be in direct competition with each other. So, with NCL's announcement that they had bought the huge former French flagship, Carnival were forced to act quickly if they wanted to retain their position in the market. With the *Windsor Castle* unavailable to them and no other suitable second hand tonnage for sale, Carnival were faced with having to place an order for a new ship: an extreme step, since they had only just taken delivery of *Festivale*.

The contract to build Carnival's first new ship was placed with the Danish shipyard Aalborg Vaerft A/S. She was launched as *Tropicale*, in an almost completed state, on the 31st October, 1980 and was delivered in December, 1980 and was delivered in December, 1980, entering service in January, 1981. In just nine years, Carnival had gone from being a fragile, one-ship company on the brink of bankruptcy to taking delivery of a purpose-built 23,000 gross ton cruise ship.

Even the attraction of a brand new addition to the Carnival fleet could not dim the enduring popularity of *Mardi Gras* and *Carnivale*. Early in 1982, *Mardi Gras* was extensively refurbished: unfortunately, in rather questionable taste in some areas. The Showboat Lounge, once upon a time the First Class St. Lawrence Club had initially been re-decorated by Carnival in red-flocked wallpaper and with very traditional red and gold drapes over her windows, creating an intimate atmosphere. Now, the room was opened up by the removal of large pillars on either side of the dance floor and was refurnished with light weight bent-wood café-style chairs, while the drapes were removed. The windows were replaced with vividly coloured stained glass-effect panels that seemed curiously at odds with the original cocktail bar and the ceiling lighting arrangements, which had been retained. Elsewhere through the ship, new furnishings, carpets and draperies were installed. The work included the refinishing of much of her panelling and in the Carousel Lounge, zebra wood now replaced the Formica wall panels. A flashing light system was installed in the Point After disco, apparently to give it a 'tropical' feeling! In November, *Carnivale* was also refurbished in similar style.

With the introduction of *Tropicale*, Carnival had broadened their horizons by positioning her on cruises out of Los Angeles and they made further adjustments to the itineraries of the Caribbean ships. Both *Mardi Gras* and *Carnivale* were occasionally diverted from Miami to make cruises to Bermuda from Boston or Philadelphia, or from Baltimore or Norfolk. Then, from the 25th May, 1984, *Carnivale* began operating 3-day cruises from Miami to Nassau and 4-day cruises to Freeport and Nassau. For those passengers just looking to party, these short cruises were ideal and were reminiscent of the 'cruises to nowhere' that she had operated out of New York for Greek Line. Particularly popular was her 4 pm Friday sailing, arriving Nassau at 9am the following day. She would sail from there at 8am on Sunday and the rest of the day was spent in very leisurely cruising back to Miami, though the activity on board was no doubt hectic. She docked at 7 am on Monday, in time for her Miami-based passengers to get in to work: doubtless somewhat hungover! *Mardi Gras* was moved to a western Caribbean itinerary, calling at Cozumel, Grand Cayman and Ocho Rios.

In 1984, *Carnivale* underwent further refurbishment to make her even more suited to the 'party' nature of her short cruises. The Riverboat Lounge and the Riverboat Casino, the former Tourist Class Lounge and Smoking Room, were merged to become one large casino. The cocktail bar, which had until then retained its intimate original proportions – and was therefore far too small for the fun-seeking crowd the ship was aimed at – was enlarged and extended into what had been the enclosed promenade.

The Arison winning formula continued, so that by 1989 *Mardi Gras, Carnivale, Festivale* and *Tropicale* had been joined by three more new ships: *Holiday, Jubilee* and *Celebration*, all well over 46,000 gross tons. The company was now being marketed as 'The Most Popular Cruise Line in the World'. While *Carnivale* continued to maintain her 3- and 4-day cruises out of Miami, *Mardi Gras* was repositioned to Fort Lauderdale and also placed in the 3- and 4-day cruise market. This was the area of cruising that showed the greatest potential for expansion. In 1985, *Mardi Gras*, too, had undergone a further refurbishment during which the cocktail bar in her Carousel Lounge, the one-time Tourist Class Windsor Lounge, was expanded through into the enclosed promenade, in the same way as the bar aboard *Carnivale* had been.

It was remarkable to consider that in 1989, after seventeen years under the Carnival banner during which time the cruise industry had changed out of all recognition, nothing had been done to alter the overall appearance of *Mardi Gras*. She was flawlessly maintained, internally and externally, but she still presented the same *Empress of Canada* profile. In some internal areas, work had even been done to remove the tacky silver foil wallpaper and to restore her rich panelling of Empire woods to the original lustrous glory of her Canadian Pacific days. Some of the new furnishings, particularly in the Main Lounge, were complimentary to the original style of the ship. The arrangement of her public spaces remained almost the same and nothing had been attempted to create a more expansive lido area, for example. However, one thing had been done that was a considerable aid to her operation: the fitting of a diesel-driven bow-thruster, which aided her manoeuvrability and lessened her dependence on tugs. This had been done following the successful operation of a similar unit fitted to *Festivale* during her conversion in 1978.

In 1989, with their new *Fantasy* nearing completion, Carnival gave serious consideration to the idea of selling *Carnivale*, thinking that she no longer fitted into their world of glittering mega-liners. They even went as far as inviting tenders for her. Apparently, they were also giving some thought to the possibility of expanding their operations to the Australian market and, perhaps, basing her on South Pacific cruises out of Sydney. But, having reconsidered these ideas, they announced that from the 9th February, 1990, *Carnivale* would be repositioned to Port Canaveral, but still on the Nassau and Freeport run. In preparation for this, and to make her more able to compete against Premier Cruises' newer and highly regarded *StarShip Atlantic* and *StarShip Oceanic*, *Carnivale* was given a $12 million, 6-week refit.

The work was carried out while she was alongside at Miami during the end of December and through January. Several hundred marble tiles were fitted to the Dining Room floor and elsewhere in the ship. The design of the refurbishment was the responsibility of Joe Farcus, who had already amazed everyone with his remarkable use of colour, lighting effects, different reflective surfaces and imaginatively themed interiors on Carnival's new ships. Mr. Farcus said of the *Carnivale* refurbishment that "It was a challenge to take this veteran ship and breathe new life into her, to create the same interest and excitement as found aboard Carnival's three superliners." In the cavernous spaces of the vast new ships, his designs were

nothing short of inspired but they just did not seem to work within the confines of a vessel that still exuded a North Atlantic liner sensibility. In places, some of her vintage panelling and fittings were restored but elsewhere they were either replaced or, as in the case of cabin fixtures, they were painted over in a speckled purple and red effect.

When, in January, 1990, Carnival took delivery of the 70,000 gross ton *Fantasy*, it was difficult to imagine that only eighteen years earlier the 27,259 gross ton *Mardi Gras* had been the largest ship sailing from Miami. Towards the end of the year, Carnival announced that they would transfer *Mardi Gras* to join *Carnivale* in Port Canaveral. In fact, *Carnivale*'s cruises from that port had proved to be such a success, often booked to capacity, that she and *Mardi Gras* ran on identical itineraries. Also, operating the two oldest ships of the fleet together meant that they could not be contrasted with the new large ships that the company wanted to be identified with.

Mardi Gras and *Carnivale* were both scheduled to sail from Port Canaveral at 5.30 pm on Thursdays, arriving in Nassau at 1 pm on Friday. They remained there overnight, departing at 6 am on Saturday and arriving back in Port Canaveral at 7 am Sunday morning. By 5.30pm, again fully loaded with fun-seeking party-goers, they set sail on another cruise, this time to Freeport, where they remained from 8 am until 4 pm on Monday. At 7 am on Tuesday they arrived at Nassau, departing at 6 am the following morning. Both ships were once again alongside at Port Canaveral by 7 am on Thursday. Throughout, they sailed in convoy, never out of sight of each other. As the cruises were of no great distance, they steamed at little more than 12 knots. It seems that *Carnivale* was able to steam more slowly than *Mardi Gras*, with the result that on occasions *Mardi Gras* had to sail in circles around her sister. Little was provided in the way of planned entertainment during the 'sea days', the focus of the ships being the casinos and slot machines.

Carnival did not just regard Port Canaveral as a convenient location for their two outmoded cruise ships, however. They were interested in the contract that Premier Cruise Lines had with the Walt Disney organisation. Carnival's marketing was nothing short of perfect, for while *Mardi Gras* and *Carnivale* were by then regarded as vintage liners, nowhere in the same league as most of the ships in the Caribbean area, they nevertheless made such an impact on the Port Canaveral/Bahamas run that Premier Cruise Lines announced in early 1991 that they were putting their expansion plans on hold and they revised their pricing in a direct response to Carnival's entry into their market. Carnival responded by putting together a deal to acquire Premier, and there were rumours that they would expand the area of Premier's operations to include a cruise service out of a Californian port: and that *Mardi Gras* would be the ship they used. Unfortunately, the plan to acquire Premier collapsed and the two lines continued to compete in the Port Canaveral trade.

While Carnival had been adding new and ever larger ships to their fleet, they had also set their sights on expansion within the cruise industry. In January, 1989, they had bought the highly respected Holland America Line, whose main areas of operation were Alaska and the Caribbean. Now, with the finances of Carnival behind them, Holland America were able to move into other

Carnival became noted for its immaculate, well-run ships. *Mardi Gras* **is seen here at Nassau in the Bahamas.** *Author's collection.*

cruising areas, such as Europe and Asia. Nevertheless, Carnival wanted to enter the European market on a larger scale and in the summer of 1992 they started discussions with the French company Club Med concerning a possible joint venture. Considerable progress was made and the two companies reached a point where it was agreed that either *Mardi Gras* or *Carnivale* would be positioned in the Mediterranean in the Spring of 1993. They were also reported to be exploring ways to start a mass-market operation in Asia. Club Med, being a better-known name in Europe, would promote the cruises. Then, suddenly, it was announced that these plans had been put back a full year. Club Med had just taken delivery of their second sail-assisted cruise ship and were rather deeply involved in promoting their own style of cruise product rather than taking on the responsibility of someone else's. In the end, the joint venture never developed any further.

By the end of 1992, Carnival once again turned their attention back to the American market and now openly expressed their interest in taking over Premier's rôle of 'The Official Cruise Line of Walt Disney World', with passengers being offered a vacation there together with a 3- or 4-day cruise. Premier had held the contract since June, 1989 and, while it was set to run for ten years, either party could terminate the agreement after June, 1994. Hence Carnival's move into Premier's territory with the

transfer of *Mardi Gras* and *Carnivale* to Port Canaveral. However, this plan also failed to develop any further as the Disney organisation were themselves beginning to look at the possibility of moving into the cruise industry.

Carnival remained in the mood for expansion, however, and they again looked to the Orient. There were indications that they had ideas about operating *Mardi Gras* on cruises out of Japan and running *Carnivale* out of Singapore. However, this seems to have been purely an investigation into the cruise market in those areas and the two 'Empresses' remained in the Port Canaveral service. It was interesting, however, that the company, which by now was well-known for its large purpose-built cruise ships, should have considered using the former trans-Atlantic liners to spearhead moves into new markets. In fact, these various ideas and projects involving the former 'Empresses' generated rumours that Carnival were anxious to dispose of them and that they were likely to be sold for scrap. Carnival, of course, vigorously denied any such intention.

Even without additional expansion into other markets, Carnival were generating a remarkable level of business. In 1992, the company had record earnings and the 18 ships that made up the entire Carnival empire carried 1.1 million passengers, an increase of 5 per cent over the previous year. Early in 1993, Carnival made it known that they had taken a record number of 68,676 bookings in the week from the 4th to the 10th January and an unprecedented single-day total of 14,585 on the 11th.

At the same time, they announced that they would be launching a new subsidiary company, FiestaMarina Cruises, aimed strictly at the Spanish-speaking markets in Latin America, Puerto Rico, the U.S.A. and Spain. Beginning on the 22nd October, 1993, *Carnivale*, with the new name *FiestaMarina*, would sail from San Juan to St.Thomas, La Guaira, Aruba and Santo Domingo. All the services aboard the ship would be in the Spanish and Portuguese languages only. In order to give the cruises as wide an appeal as possible, there was to be the opportunity for passengers to board the ship at La Guaira, thus dividing the 7-day itinerary into either 3- or 4-day segments if preferred. *Carnivale*'s place on the Port Canaveral run was to be taken by the large, nearly new *Fantasy*. Both the former 'Empresses' had by this time been in the Carnival fleet for over twenty years and were beginning to look seriously outmoded. This was particularly apparent when *Mardi Gras* was sailing alongside *Fantasy*. Carnival were therefore looking to find alternative employment for them both – hence the FiestaMarine Cruises concept, which was regarded by some in the industry as a smart move by Carnival. There was every expectation that *Mardi Gras*, and possibly *Festivale*, would eventually join the renamed *Carnivale* in this new operation.

However, just a few months after the announcement, Carnival issued a further statement regarding the future of *Mardi Gras*. She was to be sold to a new concern in which Carnival, Dolphin Cruise Line and the famous Greek shipping company Epirotiki Lines would have equal interests and which would operate cruises in the Eastern Mediterranean. Carnival had not lost sight of their aim to penetrate the European market and this move was seen as a way of getting a toe-hold there. After some refitting work, the ship was to be operated by Epirotiki under the Greek flag as *Olympic* and her cruises would be marketed to both North American and European passengers beginning in March, 1994. In the meantime, still as *Mardi Gras*, she would maintain her programme of cruises from Port Canaveral until the 5th September, 1993, after which she would depart for Greece.

Thus, the problem of what to do with the two older ships seemed to have been solved – except that by the latter part of 1993 everything seemed to have changed. First, the joint venture arrangement between Carnival, Dolphin and Epirotiki was abandoned. Instead, Carnival had decided to exchange *Mardi Gras* for a small equity interest in Epirotiki. But, in fact, the two companies were already deeply involved in discussions that would result in a merger. Carnival were very focussed on establishing themselves in the European cruising market and, eventually, in a complex financial manoeuvre, they attained a 43 per cent share of Epirotiki Lines in exchange for both the former *Mardi Gras* and the former *Carnivale*. *Carnivale* was, of course, due to sail as the *FiestaMarina* and she would continue to do so, but now under bareboat charter from Epirotiki with Carnival operating her with their own crew. It was a curious marriage: the all-powerful, vigorous and still relatively new company, Carnival, and the long-established, very traditional family firm of Epirotiki.

Then, further change came with the announcement by Epirotiki that *Mardi Gras* would not be sailing in the Mediterranean as *Olympic* after all. The Eastern Mediterranean cruise market was going through a decline, so instead they took the opportunity to place her on what appeared to be a potentially lucrative charter elsewhere. On the 30th September, Peter J. Catalano, chairman of Gold Star Cruises, based in Galveston, Texas, announced that they had secured a charter of *Mardi Gras*, which they would rename *Star of Texas*. She would operate ten 'cruises to nowhere' each week: four six-hour cruises and six 'nightclub' cruises.

Mr. Catalano had ambitious plans for the former Carnival veteran, referring to her as 'the World's largest and most beautifully appointed day cruise ship that will usher in a new era for Galveston as a major passenger ship destination.' He went on to say, "We have intentionally taken our time to identify the right vessel to become a main attraction for Galveston." A press release commented: "Luxury cruises have traditionally been the vacation of choice for those wanting to relax away from the stress of daily rigours." Of course, it was not pointed out that, in general, passengers aboard luxury cruise ships have more than six hours to enjoy their vacation of choice! Nevertheless, the press release went on to promise: "....world-renowned performers, glamorous show-girls, big bands, magicians and comedians. The *Star of Texas* welcomes you to call in advance for onboard weddings,

In 1993, Carnival launched FiestaMarina Cruises, aimed exclusively at the Spanish-speaking market and using *Carnivale*, now re-named *FiestaMarina*. *Author's collection.*

After a long and successful career with Carnival, *Mardi Gras* was less fortunate during her charter to a new company, Gold Star Cruises, as *Star of Texas*. *Andres Hernandez collection*.

business meetings, lectures or charity gala events. Weekly attractions include Monday 'Sports Nights' and Wednesday 'Ladies Nights' cruises. Two-day getaway cruises to Mexico will occur monthly and special holiday-theme cruises such as Mardi Gras or Valentine's voyages will be offered throughout the year." On the 30th October, 1993, *Star of Texas* sailed from Galveston on the first of these outings.

Meanwhile, on the 18th October, a brilliantly clear, sunny day at the port of Miami, Miss Universe, the 18 year-old Dayanara Torres from Puerto Rico, performed the ceremony re-naming *Carnivale* as *FiestaMarina*. Although now a 38 year-old vessel and a long-familiar sight in Miami, she was given all the fanfare normally accorded to a new ship, with two tugs escorting her into the port. Although now operated by a Carnival subsidiary, FiestaMarina Cruises, she still carried the parent company's distinctive colours on her funnel. However, the name *FiestaMarina* was emblazoned on either side of her bow in large free-form script, in red of course! Such superficial glitz was not enough to ensure success, however. And neither was Mr. Catalano's hyperbole for Gold Star Cruises.

After twenty years of popularity and success, both former 'Empresses' now found themselves in the unfamilar waters of unpopularity and failure. After barely three months of running *FiestaMarina* out of San Juan, FiestaMarina Cruises announced that they would reposition her to Miami from June, 1994 following disappointing sales in the Latin marketplace. Apparently, most Latins from South American countries enjoy visiting Miami, so it was decided that this would be a more natural base for the ship. The fact that *FiestaMarina*'s fares were drastically reduced – the lead-in fare being only $399, a $500 reduction from the original brochure rate – was a sure indication that her cruises were not selling well. On the 29th April, she sailed on her final cruise from San Juan, after which she entered dry-dock for refurbishment before resuming her cruises, now from Miami. The itinerary had been revised so that she now called at the Dominican Republic port of Samana, then at San Juan and St. Thomas.

Gold Star Cruises soon ran into financial difficulties, reportedly losing over $4½ million in just eleven months. On the 9th November, 1994, *Star of Texas* was moved from Galveston to Miami. With the singularly inappropriate new name of *Lucky Star* (but still with *Star of Texas* painted on her stern), she continued operating cruises of just a few hours' duration: twelve sailings each

week, ostensibly as a gambling vessel. *Mardi Gras*, once the toast of the port of Miami and the ship that helped shape the cruise industry, was in much reduced circumstances! One of her mid-week cruises was priced at just $19.95, which made her previous $49 cruises out of Galveston appear very up-market indeed. Her operators were nevertheless 'up-beat' about the idea and were talking of acquiring a smaller ship for use out of Galveston. The operation seemed to last but a moment, however: it had got off to a bad start, having been disrupted by a tropical storm. Ultimately, *Lucky Star* failed because she was too large for day cruises and offered poorly scheduled cruises, with two of her weekend trips not returning to Miami until 3 am. The operation was closed down on the 30th December, after its parent companies filed for bankruptcy protection in New York. Gold Star Cruises of Galveston and Lucky Star Cruises of Miami had not generated enough income to pay the $600,000 monthly lease for the ship and crew. Consequently, *Lucky Star* was repossessed by her owners, Epirotiki, and was ordered away from Miami owing debts of over $300,000.

Likewise, the FiestaMarina concept was not, after all, the smart move that some cruise industry watchers had conceived it to be. For once, Carnival had misjudged the market. *FiestMarina* sailed from Miami on the 4th September, 1994 on her final cruise for the company and, on her return on the 11th, Carnival shut down its FiestaMarina organisation. Apparently, many people in the Spanish-speaking market were already veteran cruise passengers and were familiar with the slick new cruise ships that were beginning to proliferate throughout the Caribbean: so they had not taken kindly to being 'fobbed-off' with a vessel which was clearly Carnival's cast-off. FiestaMarina Cruises had only run for ten months.

Once more under Greek control, *FiestaMarina* sailed from Miami on the 14th September for the Mediterranean (as *Mardi Gras* had been expected to do before she became *Star of Texas*). The somewhat pretentious *FiestaMarina* identity was removed and she was given the altogether more dignified name of *Olympic*. Epirotiki Lines announced that, following a refurbishment, she would begin operating 7-day cruises from Piraeus to Istanbul,

11

Empresses in Europe

The former *FiestaMarina* emerged from the refit that had transformed her into *Olympic* looking even more handsome than she ever had before. She now had a pale buff-coloured hull with a dark blue sheer line and a dark blue funnel bearing the combined logos of both Epirotiki and Sun Lines. The alliance between Epirotiki and Carnival had been quickly dissolved when it became clear that it was not going to be a partnership that would benefit either party and, instead, Epirotiki had merged with Sun Lines in December, 1994 under the name Royal Olympic Cruises. (*Olympic* was actually registered under the ownership of Turquoise Sea Shipping). As a result of the divorce from Carnival, Epirotiki, or Royal Olympic as it became, was left with the two 'Empresses', ships somewhat larger than anything they had owned and operated in the past. True, they had, rather surprisingly, acquired the 20,000 gross ton *Carla C.* from Costa Line in 1992 but she had been destroyed by fire early in 1994, after only a brief career with them.

Not only did *Olympic*'s new livery suit her very well but she was in impeccable condition, having been flawlessly maintained by Carnival over the years. To better reflect her return to Greek ownership, her decks and public rooms were now given names that recalled Greek mythology. Sun and Sports Decks became Zeus and Leda Decks; Promenade Deck was now Hera Deck; Empress Deck was Apollo Deck; and Upper, Main and Riviera Decks were named Venus, Dionysos and Poseidon Decks. Also, as part of the refit, two of the four pools on the lido deck were removed and were replaced by a jacuzzi.

Ship historian Peter Knego boarded the ship on the 1st August, 1997 for a 3-day Aegean cruise and was very impressed by what he found: "*Olympic*'s public rooms are a mix of vintage Canadian Pacific and 1990 Carnival Cruises glitz. Hera Deck begins with the delightful Nine Muses nightclub, a semi-circular space with an original bamboo-lined bar, recessed white plaster ceiling, rich wooden panelling, heavy brass doors and etched glass windows along its aft bulkhead. Chrome-framed chairs and vividly-coloured carpeting appear to be from the 1990 refit. The cinema Theatron, further aft, remains thankfully untouched from the *Empress of Britain* era. It is a study in polished wood and leather-trimmed bulkheads, plaster acoustic ceiling and vivid red seating. The Sirenes Show Lounge encompasses the stern. Its partly-themed décor also dates to Carnival's 1990 refit. The entire deck is fringed by promenades lined with floor to ceiling windows. These promenades were once sedate linoleum-covered passages lined with steamer chairs. In 1990, they were 'dressed up' with black, white and red chequered Formica panelling, bright yellow lights and hot pink and purple sofas.

"The Dining Room is down on Dionysos Deck and retains its original layout, although the rich wood panelling

Once again under Greek ownership, as during her days as *Queen Anna Maria*, *Carnivale* became Royal Olympic Cruises' *Olympic*. *Kevin M. Anthoney.*

and pillars have been replaced with multi-coloured, light-bulb trimmed Formica. One deck down, forward on Poseidon Deck, the Olympia pool and sauna area is largely unchanged from the ship's trans-Atlantic days. Our cabin, ASU44, was located on the starboard side of Apollo Deck and had two large brass-framed windows, a separate toilet, large bathroom and two very high beds. In some places, the panelling was beautifully polished, while in others it was disguised by purple and mauve paint."

Olympic was employed on a 3-day itinerary, which departed from Piraeus on Friday mornings, calling at Mykonos, Rhodes, Kusadasi and Patmos during the weekend and returning to Piraeus at 7 am on Monday. Just four hours later, she would depart on a 4-day cruise, with calls at Mykonos, Kusadasi, Patmos, Rhodes, Heraklion and Santorini. It was during one of these cruises, on the 6th April, 1997, that she damaged her bow when she struck a wharf while manoeuvring at Kusadasi. The Turkish officials demanded guarantees equivalent to $3 million for repairs to the berth before allowing her to sail the following day.

Despite some initial concerns regarding both her size and her age – the line had hitherto only used ships of less than half her tonnage on Aegean cruises; and she was by then 41 years old – *Olympic* began to settle well into her new rôle. In fact, such was her success that there was some speculation that her near-sister, then languishing in lay-up, might join her.

Lucky Star had indeed proved to be a choice of name that tempted fate – luck had certainly not smiled upon the former *Mardi Gras*. She had been placed in lay-up for a while in Freeport in the Bahamas but then, sensing that there was no longer a future for her in the Caribbean, Royal Olympic had her taken over to the Mediterranean. She arrived in Piraeus on the 10th May, 1995. However, there was no rôle for her there either and she was laid up in Eleusis pending a decision on repairs and refitting. During this time, her name was changed to *Apollon*, although there was for a time talk of her returning to service as the *Homeric* and at one stage *Olympic 2004* was painted on her bows.

All reports were that she had been somewhat abused by her charterer and by the passengers her cheap cruises of just a few hours had attracted. Several companies expressed some interest in acquiring her for further sailing but, upon inspection, seemed to find the prospect of restoring her rather daunting. One did, however, appear to be willing to take her on: they were known as Royal Venture Cruises and had plans to charter *Apollon* for a series of Caribbean cruises beginning on the 14th July, 1996. However, Royal Venture, who had already attempted to start operations with another vessel, had to drop the plan as there were outstanding liens against the ship in both Florida and Texas, which meant that she would have been seized as soon as she arrived there. There were also rumours at the time indicating a return to Canadian waters, under charter to a Canadian firm, but this likewise failed to develop. It seemed, therefore, that the former *Empress of Canada* was at the end of her career and that, perhaps after several years of idleness and slipping further into disrepair, she would be towed to some distant breaker's yard.

In the mid-1990s, cruise bookings were on the increase, particularly in the United Kingdom. There, the market rose 22 per cent from 352,000 in 1995 to 429,000 passengers in 1996. This expansion was largely boosted by growth at the lower end of the market: essentially the sector that Carnival had developed in America in the 1970s. While there had been mass-market cruising in Europe and the U.K. during that same period, it had not developed at the same pace as in the United States. Now, several tour operators who had previously concentrated on land-based package holidays began to diversify into the cruise market. Whereas cruises had more traditionally been aimed at the middle-aged and older, the new entrants were targeting more youthful age groups, including young families. At the forefront of this expansion were Airtours and Thomsons. Thomsons had, in fact, briefly played quite a significant rôle in U.K. cruising in the early-1970s and now, after a twenty year absence, made a comeback in 1996. This was doubtless to some extent inspired by the success of the two-ship operation of Airtours. While Airtours had elected to acquire their own fleet, redundant 'first generation' vessels from Royal Caribbean, Thomson chose to tread a little more carefully and charter their ships. Their first was the 12,218 gross ton *Sapphire*.

It was an unfortunate return to cruising, as they were forced to suspend the newly-launched programme after only two trips when *Sapphire*, which they had chartered from the Cyprus-based Louis Cruise Lines, suffered engine failure. After she was repaired and resumed cruising, she was joined by another Louis Cruise Lines vessel, *Emerald*. This ship had begun life as the American *Santa Rosa*, owned by Grace Line. Her active career had not been a long one and she had spent eighteen years in lay-up before being acquired by the rapidly expanding Regency Cruises. They had her totally rebuilt, so that she was almost a brand new ship. In November, 1995, Regency collapsed into bankruptcy and five of its six vessels were impounded by creditors. Louis had managed to extract *Emerald* from the tangle of legal red tape and she became very popular with Thomson passengers. In 1996, Carnival Cruise Lines had disposed of *Festivale* to Dolphin Cruise Line and in 1997 she, too, was taken on charter by Thomson, still carrying her Dolphin name, *Island Breeze*. Based in the Mediterranean in the summer and the Caribbean during the winter, the Thomson ships became very popular and, after just one year of operation, the company began looking for a fourth vessel.

In their brochure covering the winter of 1997 through to the autumn of 1998, Thomsons stated: ".....we don't intend to rest on our oars, enjoying the praise we have received for our ships and itineraries. Instead, we have roamed the seas looking for a ship worthy of joining *Sapphire*, *Emerald* and *Island Breeze*. We believe we have found one of the best: she joins our fleet in May, 1998 as

Topaz." She had begun life as the luxurious flagship of the Swedish American Line, *Gripsholm*. In 1985, she had become *Regent Sea*, flagship of Regency Cruises. However, like most of the Regency fleet, she was laid up, entangled in litigation, and despite any negotiations that Thomson had entered into, she remained thus. Very quickly, Thomson issued a further brochure featuring another, very different but equally lovely vessel with the name *Topaz*.

Even though *Olympic* had experienced some measure of success cruising the Aegean for Royal Olympic, they had found her rather too large, as well as too old – despite her good structural and mechanical condition. They were also looking to improve their fleet with new ships and, not long after the formation of the company, they had indicated that both *Olympic* and *Apollon* would be quickly replaced by new vessels. So, almost from the moment that she had joined their fleet, *Olympic* had been available for sale. As in the past, she was quick to find a buyer and at the end of her 1997 season she was sold to a Panamanian-registered company, Topaz International. This had been set up to own this one ship and the person behind it was Captain Paris Katsoufis. He had formerly been the head of Dolphin Cruise Line since its formation in 1984 and of their subsidiary Majesty Cruise Line since 1992. Then, on the 1st July, 1997, he had joined Cunard Line as President and Chief Operating Officer.

On the 19th January, 1998, still with the name

In 1998, *Olympic* became *Topaz*. Although not devoid of modern equipment, her bridge was the most wonderful period piece. *Peter Knego.*

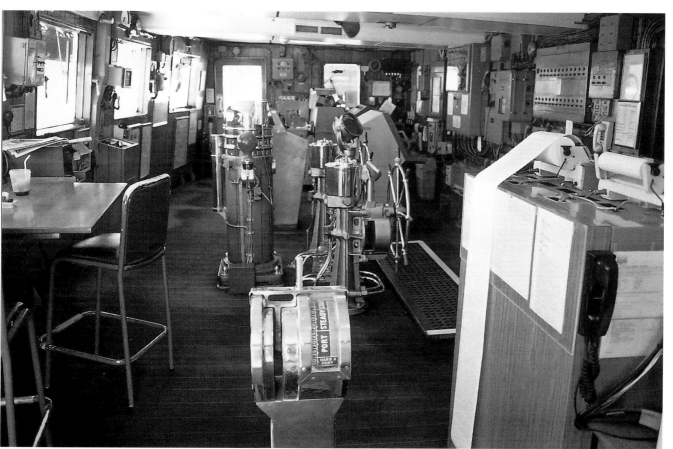

Olympic, the ship was taken to the Skaramanga shipyards to undergo a refit before entering service as *Topaz*. It would prove to be her most radical refit since she was transformed from *Empress of Britain* into *Queen Anna Maria*. When Thomson had first announced the introduction of the former *Gripsholm* as the *Topaz*, they had also unveiled what they claimed to be a new concept: the 'all-inclusive' cruise. This included 'round the clock' dining and the creation of a cabaret restaurant. The concept was to continue aboard the refitted *Olympic* and, in fact, the layout of her public rooms meant that she was more suited to what Thomson had in mind.

When she emerged from Skaramanga as *Topaz*, she presented a new profile. Her main public room deck had been extended forward, with the new structure containing 28 cabins. Although this extension had been created with considerable care, following her sheer and incorporating curves that echoed the general lines of the rest of her superstructure, there is no denying that it did compromise her otherwise attractive profile. It meant the removal of her twin king posts, which left her looking rather empty forward. A further alteration, which went some way towards balancing the forward addition, was the creation of The Yacht Club, a restaurant above the aft nightclub which had been added back in the *Queen Anna Maria* days. The Yacht Club was given large windows in the same style as those encircling the nightclub and above it there were glazed screens, again in the same style, to shelter the new sun deck. The Yacht Club was *Topaz*'s 24-hour dining facility. The cinema, while decoratively remaining little changed, became Le Cabaret Restaurant. The seating arrangement was altered, although it was still in rows facing forward to the stage, but each row of seats now had long tables in front of it. What had long ago been the Tourist Class Lounge was transformed into a shopping arcade. Otherwise, the ship remained largely unchanged with much of Joe Farcus's insensitive 1990 refurbishment remaining intact.

Once more, the ship was wearing a new livery: whilst

not as attractive as that of Royal Olympic, it was nevertheless very pleasing and well-suited to a cruise ship. In the space between Main and A Decks there were three broad strips of blue, yellow and red along her hull, following her sheer. Three stripes of these same colours were painted diagonally across her now white funnel. In fact, these appeared to be too narrow for such a large and imposing funnel structure. While known as *Topaz*, the ship carried the seemingly unnecessary addition of the word *The* in front of her name on both her bow and her stern.

Topaz's first cruise was an 18-night trans-Atlantic crossing to Port Canaveral, an echo of her days as *Queen Anna Maria*. She was scheduled to depart Piraeus on Friday, the 17th April, 1998 and to call at Valletta, Malaga, Gibraltar, Funchal, Ponta Delgada and Bermuda. Not only was the cruise sold by Thomsons, but also by Voyages of Discovery and this latter company mentioned in their literature that *Topaz* was the former *Empress of Britain*. Even though well over thirty years had passed since she had sailed under that name, the Canadian Pacific reputation was still strong enough to be promoted.

Sadly, her re-entry into service was marred by bad publicity generated by passenger complaints. It seems that the final stages of the refit had been hurried in order to be completed on schedule and her new crew had not had sufficient time to familiarise themselves with the ship. As a result, by the time *Topaz* arrived in Malta, the Thomson representatives had received many complaints of problems with meals, poor service and apparently run-down facilities. Given Carnival's exemplary maintenance of the ship and the fact that she had just emerged from an extensive refit, the criticism of the facilities seemed to be a curious complaint. Nevertheless, Thomsons decided to remove from the ship all the 756 passengers who had booked with them. The 170 who had booked through Voyages of Discovery remained aboard to complete the rest of the cruise and by all accounts had a wonderful time as the crew became more familiar with the ship. Thomsons had devised five different itineraries for *Topaz* in the

Western Caribbean and it was their intention to operate her there year-round.

Meanwhile, at around the time that Thomsons were introducing the *Topaz* all-inclusive product, another British operator entered the cruise market: Direct Cruises. This company had been established by the direct-sell package tour company Direct Holidays and in August, 1997 advertised its first programme of cruises. These were principally aimed at potential passengers in the north of England and in Scotland. Earlier in the year, the former Costa Line flagship *Eugenio Costa* had been sold to a British company, Lowline, and had been renamed *Edinburgh Castle*. She was the ship that Direct Cruises were to use. Her cruises were mostly to be of 14 days duration and, while most of them were either to the Atlantic islands or the Western Mediterranean, two were scheduled to head northwards: one to the Norwegian fjords and the other to Iceland and Greenland. The programme was set to run between mid-April and late-October, 1998. Public reaction was overwhelming and three-quarters of the cruises were sold out within just a few weeks of the programme being announced. Buoyed by this response, Direct Cruises realised that a second ship was essential.

Toward the end of December, 1997, they announced that they had secured a five-year charter of *Apollon* from Royal Olympic Cruises, to supplement the virtually sold-out programme to be operated by *Edinburgh Castle*. With the report of the charter came the announcement that *Apollon* would undergo a $20 million repair and refurbishment before beginning service and there were

briefly rumours that she would be renamed *Stirling Castle*. Charming though this might have been, the name *Apollon* was retained. Her first cruise was scheduled to depart Piraeus for the U.K. on the 23rd April, 1998. If the introduction of the elegant former *Eugenio Costa* into the British cruise market was not exciting enough, the news that the former *Empress of Canada* was returning home after an absence of twenty-six years was positively spectacular, especially as she would once again be sailing from the River Mersey. By this time, she had spent over two idle years at her Eleusis Bay anchorage. Like her near-sister, she was to undergo her refurbishment work at the Skaramanga shipyard.

Unfortunately, the Direct Cruises operation got off to a bad start. After brief use as a casino ship in the United States, *Edinburgh Castle* arrived to be made ready at the Cammell Laird shipyard at Birkenhead on the 31st March, 1998. About 30 passengers refused to travel on her first Direct Cruises sailing after a burst pipe flooded several cabins. Direct Cruises made arrangements to transfer them to *Apollon*'s first cruise from Liverpool but this had to be cancelled pending necessary repairs to her boilers. Shortly after leaving the Mediterranean on her way to Britain, she had suffered a reduction in speed and had reported boiler damage. She was diverted to Avonmouth for repairs, arriving there on the 5th May. A further problem was that some of the refurbishment work, which should have been completed during the voyage, was halted as workmen became ill owing to the stormy conditions encountered as *Apollon* slowly made her way up the Portuguese coast and through the Bay of Biscay.

Now with broader blue, yellow and red bands on her funnel, the enduring *The Topaz* is seen during a visit to Malta. *Author.*

111

Two ships under charter to Thomson Cruises, *The Emerald* and *The Topaz*, make a fine sight. Visible behind them are the funnels of the much bigger *Costa Victoria*. *Author.*

Consequently, several of her cruises had to be cancelled to allow sufficient time for all the work to be completed. She eventually arrived in the Mersey on the 30th May, to begin her first cruise from Liverpool for twenty-seven years.

Although tied up alongside the shabby Langton Dock instead of in the shadow of the majestic Liver Building, *Apollon* still managed to create enough magic to make her passengers, and curious onlookers, believe that they had stepped back into the 1960s. Her profile, apart from the removal of all but two of her cargo-handling derricks, remained the same as when she had last been berthed there. Now, her formidable funnel was dark blue and carried the circular logo of Royal Olympic Cruises and along her hull she bore a broad blue sheer line.

Internally, while sailing for Carnival, she had the good fortune to have escaped the kind of glitzy make-over that had been inflicted upon *Carnivale*. As a result, when her first Direct Cruises passengers went aboard, they found much of her panelling, etched glass and brass-work intact. Behind the orchestra stand in the main lounge, the balustrade to the sweeping staircase leading up to the balcony still had the entwined letters CP ornately worked into it, while the balcony rail retained its stylised maple leaf motif. What had once been the aft-facing Banff Club had, during the ship's days with Carnival, been the disco and its attractively panelled walls had been painted black. Perhaps the black paint was too difficult, or too time-consuming, to remove – it had again been painted, but this time in pale lavender. The graciously proportioned former First Class lounge was still fitted out as a casino. (This would prove to be an unpopular spot and Direct Cruises had hopes of returning it to its original function.)

The ship's original furnishings had, of course, worn out long ago. Their replacements were for the most part attractive but there was nevertheless an impression that not enough time or money had been spent on this aspect of the ship. Even so, all traces of the effects of over two years inactivity following hard use as a casino ship had been removed. *Apollon*, in fact, looked well cared for and her passengers warmed to her. Having been built on the Tyne and based on the Mersey, now that she was back there and marketed mainly to the North, she was very much 'their ship' and her first cruises were truly an acknowledgement of that fact.

Apollon's initial cruise from the Mersey took her to Cadiz, Casablanca, the Canary Islands, Madeira and Guernsey and ended in her birthplace, Newcastle-on-Tyne. Her next cruise had a similar itinerary and returned to Newcastle, but her third cruise terminated at Greenock, where she had called many times during her days on the Canadian service. The remaining cruises of that first season were all from Greenock and took her into the Mediterranean. The final one departed Greenock on the 18th October and called at Liverpool on the following day to embark more passengers. It ended in Piraeus, her passengers being returned home by air.

It had not all been smooth sailing for Direct Cruises, however. Quite apart from *Apollon*'s disrupted introduction into service, several of *Edinburgh Castle*'s cruises were marred by technical problems. On the 24th May, with the delays to the start of *Apollon*'s programme still in the news, *Edinburgh Castle* suffered an electrical short circuit in her main switchboard soon after 1,000 passengers had embarked for a 14-day cruise. They were

given full refunds and compensation and the majority agreed to the offer of a rescheduled cruise of one week. Then in June, another cruise was disrupted due to a health scare: two former passengers had contracted legionnaires' disease. Although there was no link between this fact and the ship, Direct Cruises had the drinking water system disinfected in order to reassure passengers. These events resulted in a great deal of negative publicity, principally generated by the media rather than the passengers. (They were very enthusiastic about the ship, as I was later to discover.)

Confident that the problems with *Edinburgh Castle* would be resolved and with the expectation of selling over 20,000 cruises during the initial season, and even more in 1999, Direct Cruises had very soon begun to look towards further expansion. Briefly, there were rumours that they would charter a third ship, the former Italian liner *Ausonia*. Then, on the 21st July, an ominous announcement was made. Direct Holidays, the parent company of Direct Cruises, had been sold to Airtours for £80.7 million. Assurances were made that Direct Holidays would continue to trade as a direct-sell arm of Airtours but no mention was made regarding Direct Cruises. By this time, Airtours were poised to take delivery from Royal Caribbean of the 37,584 gross ton former *Song of America*. She would be their fourth ship, all of them aimed at the same level of the market as Direct Cruises. Airtours had,

in fact, already made a bid for Direct in 1997 and, shortly before their second and successful bid, Thomson had also attempted a take-over of the company. Competition for the expanding U.K. market was heating up.

The problems for *Edinburgh Castle* were far from over. In September, she suffered an electrical failure, causing damage to a generator. As a result, she had to put into Cadiz for repairs and her passengers were flown home. This affected the departure dates for the remaining cruises of her summer schedule. At the end of the programme, she arrived in Southampton on the 14th October for major refitting and repair work that was expected to take up to ten weeks to complete. As a result, her owners, Lowline, lost a very lucrative charter for her. On the 21st December, the Admiralty Marshal placed her under arrest due to alleged breach of contract.

Meanwhile, Direct Cruises stated that they were unhappy with the refit of *Apollon* undertaken by Royal Olympic. Direct were facing claims for compensation totalling £1 million from holidaymakers whose cruises were either cancelled or disrupted. The year 1999 brought even worse news. *Edinburgh Castle* was again arrested in January, for alleged debts, and in February she was put into receivership. It was announced that she would be sold to recoup the money outstanding. During the winter months, the repair work had been completed and Direct Cruises had fully expected her to begin her second season with

Now under charter to Direct Cruises, *Apollon* visited Oslo in July, 1999 during a memorable Baltic cruise. *Author.*

them on the 27th March, 1999. They had announced a programme of fifteen cruises by *Apollon* and fourteen by *Edinburgh Castle* between then and October. The loss of *Edinburgh Castle* was an immense blow to Direct Cruises, and to the cruising public. Although she had endured more than her fair share of problems, she had built up a loyal following – 13,500 passengers had sailed aboard her during 1998 and many were booked for 1999. As the news of *Edinburgh Castle*'s bankruptcy came at a time when it would have been difficult to find another ship for the summer, Direct Cruises announced that they would concentrate just on *Apollon* and those passengers booked to sail on *Edinburgh Castle* would be offered alternative cruises aboard her instead.

Apollon's cruises for 1999 largely followed the same routes as those operated by her and *Edinburgh Castle* during the previous year: the Atlantic islands, North Africa and the Western Mediterranean. However, the two cruises that headed north were undoubtedly the real highlights, not only of her 1999 programme but of her career. One of them took her along the Norwegian coast, deep into the beautiful fjords, up as far as the North Cape and then onward up to the dramatic scenery of Spitsbergen. It was the very first time that she had ever ventured into those waters. Not even as *Empress of Canada* had she made such a cruise. Then, on the 3rd July, she made a midnight departure from Liverpool for a cruise into the Baltic. On this 14-day voyage, she called at Oslo, Stockholm, Helsinki, St. Petersburg and Copenhagen. Surely, it can only have been by coincidence, rather than by careful planning, that on the 2nd July thirty years earlier she had sailed as *Empress of Canada* on one of her very rare cruises from Liverpool – also to the Baltic. That had been the first and only other time that she had visited that part of the World. On that occasion, she had called at Bergen, Stockholm, Helsinki and Copenhagen. So, even during her 1999 cruise programme the thirty eight year-old ship was till making 'maiden arrivals'.

Apollon's entry into Oslo was particularly memorable. It was a brilliantly hot and sunny day. Some small craft had accompanied her as she had slowly made her way up the Oslofjord and a tug with fire-fighting equipment sent up plumes of water in welcome as she manoeuvred towards her berth. To complete the picture, Norwegian Cruise Line's *Norway* was also in port, dominating the harbour, along with *Black Prince* and *Splendour of the Seas*. The final cruise of the season began on the 9th October, when *Apollon* departed Liverpool on a leisurely 13-night voyage back to Piraeus with calls in Spain, on the Riviera and in Italy.

There had at one point been the suggestion that Direct Cruises were looking for a ship to replace *Edinburgh Castle*, but when the 2000 brochure was issued it only featured *Apollon* – with several images of that glorious maiden arrival at Oslo. It was a much more ambitious programme than those for the previous two years, extending from March to November. There were several Mediterranean-based fly-cruises and cruises from other ports such as Bristol and Dublin, as well as Liverpool and Greenock. It appeared that Direct Cruises had put their troubled beginnings behind them and that *Apollon* was establishing herself well in the U.K. cruise market. Unfortunately, it was not to be. Early in 2000, Direct Cruises announced the abandonment of the entire cruise programme and the

cancellation of the charter of the *Apollon*. They cited poor bookings as the reason but, as the announcement was made so very early in the year, the hand of Airtours was all too apparent.

Once again, *Apollon* was placed in lay-up: what, had promised to be a rather splendid final career was now discarded in favour of someone's boardroom deals. There were certainly reports that all was not well between Airtours and Direct Cruises and indications that there was some form of dispute between them over the cessation of the Direct Cruises operation. This was somewhat confirmed several months later when, in January 2001, a complicated lease/purchase deal was struck between Airtours and Royal Olympic, by now known as Royal Olympia. Under the deal, Royal Olympia bareboat chartered the 800-passenger cruise ship *Seawing* from Airtours for four years but time chartered her back to Airtours for 240 days per annum for five years. At the end of the fourth year, Royal Olympia had the option to purchase her for a nominal sum. At the same time, the two companies agreed to cancel the *Apollon* charter, which, at the time the deal was struck, still had two of the original five years remaining.

Back in May, 2000, *Apollon* had been drydocked at Eleusis. From the activity around her it appeared that she was being made ready for a return to service. However, it proved to be just routine maintenance, to ensure that she remained an attractive proposition for anyone looking to charter her, and she was returned to lay-up in Perama. Once again, she was the subject of rumour and speculation. Then, at the end of 2000, Royal Olympia issued their new cruise programme for the summer of 2001 and there, amongst the eight ships featured, was a computer-enhanced image of *Apollon*. She was no longer a 'White Empress' but wore the Royal Olympia livery of dark blue hull topped by a gold stripe. She was to be employed, along with several other ships of the fleet, on 4- and 5-day cruises in the Aegean. Royal Olympia were enthusiastic about her introduction into their Aegean operation, stating that they believed her cruises would be top-selling itineraries "that will have cruising enthusiasts all over the World applauding".

The continuing problems in Israel were, however, having a serious effect on cruise bookings in the Eastern Mediterranean and it seemed for a while that *Apollon*, with her 914-passenger capacity (approximately twice that of her fleetmates) might not be needed. Very briefly, there was an exciting rumour that the two former 'Empresses' would again be reunited and that *Apollon* might be chartered to sail with *Topaz* for Thomsons. It was just a rumour and in May, 2001 *Apollon* arrived in Piraeus harbour, looking more stately than ever in her new dark-hulled livery and ready to embark her first passengers for her short cruises to the Aegean islands. In addition to these, she made one longer cruise to the Western Mediterranean, which was marketed only to Greek passengers. This was, however, a somewhat brief and disrupted return to service: in July she was chartered to be part of a remarkable array of cruise ships that would provide accommodation for the delegates and press attending the prestigious G8 summit to be held in Genoa from the 20th to the 23rd July. Other Royal Olympiaships, *Odysseus*, *Jason* and *Triton*, were also chartered, as were *Princesa Victoria*, *Calypso*, *Serenade*, *Atalante*, *Ocean*

For Direct Cruises, *Apollon* often cruised out of Liverpool, which had been her homeport during her early career as the pride of the Canadian Pacific fleet. *J. R. Clague.*

Princesa Victoria, Calypso, Serenade, Atalante, Ocean Explorer 1 and *Costa Allegra*, along with several ferries. These summits, of the World's most powerful nations, always attract a large amount of media attention; but the high levels of security surrounding this particular one, especially the housing of everyone associated with it in such a fleet of cruise ships and the fact that the port was closed to all other traffic, gave it an unprecedentedly high profile.

At the close of the event, the ships were returned to their owners and some, including *Apollon*, resumed their interrupted cruise schedules. She continued with her programme of 4- and 5-day cruises until the 17th August. Royal Olympia had found *Olympic* rather too large for Aegean cruising, so their apparent enthusiasm for *Apollon* was a little surprising and the fragile state of the cruise market did not make it any easier to fill her. As it was, she was not popular with her crew, who were used to, and much preferred, the smaller ships of the Royal Olympia fleet. It has been suggested that the only reason that the company chose to place her in service was probably to take the place of their *World Renaissance*, which was in use for an 80-day 'semester at sea' cruise which ran until the 17th August.

At the end of her series of Aegean cruises, *Apollon* remained for a few days in Piraeus harbour. Her final

cruise had been a 4-night trip around the Cycladic islands. It is believed that her owners were at the time holding negotiations to charter her as a hotel-ship for a Libyan Arab summit. For whatever reason, this did not go ahead but in September, Royal Olympia appeared to have secured another charter for her, again to provide accommodation – this time during a NATO conference that was to be held in Naples on the 26th and 27th of that month. This would undoubtedly have been more lucrative employment for the ship than continuing to run her on cruises, especially as she was very expensive to operate. However, this charter also failed to materialise. In the aftermath of the terrorist attack on the United States on the 11th September, it was decided to move the conference to Brussels.

For a short time, *Apollon* remained moored in the Bay of Naples, along with some other ships that had also been chartered, but by early October she was back in Piraeus and was soon laid up again in Eleusis. Moored alongside her was the 4,000 gross ton *Neptune*, one of several Epirotiki-owned ships that had never been absorbed into the Royal Olympia fleet. After just a few months of inactivity, it was noted that *Apollon*'s once-pristine decks were becoming faded and cracked. Royal Olympia acknowledged in February, 2002 that to re-activate her would take five or six weeks of intensive work, plus a dry

After her Direct Cruises charter ended, Royal Olympia struggled to find employment for *Apollon*, but she looked magnificent when, with a blue hull, she visited Heraklion during a brief season of cruises in 2001.
J. D. Elliott.

'White Empresses' had at last reached the end of her career. After *Neptune* was sold for scrap, two former Sun Line vessels, *Stella Oceanis* and *Stella Solaris*, now also made redundant by Royal Olympia, joined *Apollon* to await the inevitable. Both *Stella Solaris* and *Apollon* were the subject of various rumours regarding their futures, usually involving the possibility of a static rôle, but nothing came of these ideas.

By the summer of 2003, several shipowners were taking advantage of the higher prices that could be obtained for scrap metal and were selling their redundant and laid-up cruise ships to be broken up. Many famous former liners were seen heading through the Suez Canal for Alang in India, which had become one of the most prolific shipbreaking sites. On the 16th September, it was reported that Royal Olympia had sold *Apollon*, *Stella Solaris* and *Stella Oceanis* for onward delivery to Indian breakers for around $5.17 million. After two years of inactivity, but still giving the appearance of being all but ready to depart on another cruise, *Apollon* left Eleusis on the 12th November on her final voyage. It was a long, slow

affair as she did not pass through the Suez Canal until the 21st. On the 4th December, she arrived at Alang, the *Stella Oceanis* having preceded her by several days. Both ships were anchored, waiting to be hauled up onto the beach and reduced to an unrecognisable pile of scrap metal. The career of the liner that had been described as 'The Pride of the Tyne' when she entered service over 42 years earlier was at an end.

While *Apollon* had endured a somewhat chequered few years, *Topaz* sailed serenely into the hearts of many British passengers, establishing herself as one of the most popular cruise ships. While both she and *Apollon* were aimed at the same budget end of the market, Direct Cruises appeared not to have put as much money into the operation of *Apollon* as Thomsons did with *Topaz*. Thomsons, of course, already had cruise experience to fall back on and were a larger organisation. As a result, *Topaz* boasted a far more extensive array of onboard activities, along with a more lavish programme of shows and other evening entertainment. Between November, 1998 and April, 1999 she was positioned on a series of 7-day cruises calling at the Canary Islands, Madeira and Morocco. During the summer of 1999, her homeport was Palma, from where she ran on two alternating 7-day Western Mediterranean itineraries. One of her last cruises of the season was disrupted when, on the 4th October, she was hit by the Italian ferry *Vincenzo Florio* while lying alongside the passenger terminal at Naples. The ferry was new and was manoeuvring after a trial trip, when she collided with *Topaz*'s starboard side, damaging a 20 sq. metre area of her hull. The repairs were carried out at Naples, taking two days to complete.

It was at the end of the summer 1999 season that Thomsons announced that they would be cutting back on their chartered fleet, returning *Sapphire* to Louis Cruise Lines and *Island Breeze* to Premier Cruise Line – who had absorbed Dolphin Cruise Line. They planned to concentrate their cruise activities around *Topaz* and *Emerald* and take blocks of accommodation aboard ships of other lines.

On the 28th October, *Topaz* departed Palma to spend another winter cruising the Caribbean: it would be her final season in those waters that, more than any other, she could call home. Then, on the 16th April, 2000, she sailed from Santo Domingo in the Dominican Republic for San Juan, Antigua, St. Lucia, Babados, Madeira, Casablanca, Cartagena, Tarragona and Palma. It was to be, in all probability, her final trans-Atlantic voyage. From then onward, she was positioned in the Mediterranean or the Atlantic islands and Thomsons put together a programme of far more extensive cruises in the Mediterranean than she had operated for them before.

Although she had already established herself with her earlier itineraries, it was probably these Mediterranean cruises that ensured her continuing popularity and the fact that she sailed full on virtually every voyage. During the summer of 2001, her programme was extended to include 14-day trips to the Eastern Mediterranean, with calls at Istanbul and in the Greek islands. However, due to the continued political strife in Israel and the terrorist attacks on the United States in September, some of her cruises that had been scheduled to concentrate on Egypt, Lebanon and Israel had to be rearranged.

Before beginning her 2000 programme of Mediterranean cruises, *Topaz* had been overhauled, part of the work including repainting her funnel with much broader stripes, which looked far more attractive. She was destined, however, not to carry this improved livery for

long. In 2001, Thomson Holidays, of which Thomson Cruises were a part, was bought up by the German tour company TUI. As a result, the entire group of companies that had been under the Thomson umbrella now adopted the TUI corporate identity: pale blue with a red logo, which was a stylised interpretation of the letters TUI. Whilst it looked quite attractive on the tails of aircraft that once carried the profile of Britannia, it did not suit the traditional 'ocean liner' appearance of *Topaz*. Before she began her usual series of winter cruises around the Atlantic islands, scheduled to begin with her departure from Palma on the 13th December, 2001, she had to suffer the indignity of having this corporate graffiti, which resembled little more than a smiley face, painted onto her funnel. The red, yellow and blue stripes were removed from her hull and were replaced with a broad blue band, which did not follow her sheer line, just above her boot-topping. The logo and the name Thomson were also painted on her hull, mercifully small, both at a three-quarters aft point, and also on her stern.

Unattractive or not, it was sad to know that this too would be a short-lived look: in May, 2002, it was announced that the five-year charter of *Topaz* would come to an end the following May and that Thomsons would not renew it. While there was no questioning *Topaz*'s continuing popularity, there were other factors that limited just how much longer she could remain in service. The most significant of these was the new Safety of Life at Sea (SOLAS) regulations: these were scheduled to come into force before another five-year charter would have run its course.

Also, the cruise market was continuing to grow and P&O were planning to position a large, modern ship at Palma to operate 7-day cruises aimed at the same sector of the market as Thomsons. Likewise, a new joint-venture company, Island Cruises, set up by Royal Caribbean and First Choice, were also targeting the same market with their cruise ship *Island Escape*. With the best will in the World, *Topaz*, one of the oldest operational cruise ships, just could not compete. To replace her, Thomsons had negotiated to sub-charter the former Holland America Line cruise ship *Nieuw Amsterdam* from Louis Cruise Lines. She would be renamed *Thomson Spirit*, moving Thomson Cruises up to a different level in the cruise market.

12

...And the Ship Sails On

The final cruise for *Topaz* was to be from the Canary Islands to Palma, a twelve-day voyage from Lanzarote with calls at Gran Canaria, Tenerife, *La* Palma, Madeira, Lisbon, Cadiz, Almeria and Barcelona. Her departure from Lanzarote on the 23rd April, 2003 would be just three days after the forty-seventh anniversary of her departure from Liverpool on her maiden voyage to Canada. Ignominious lay-up alongside her sister now seemed almost inevitable. Then, in early November, 2002, a remarkable announcement was made that would see *Topaz* embarking upon one of the most ambitious and exciting chapters of her already eventful career. Her owners had secured a charter for her from the Japanese educational organisation Peace Boat. She was scheduled to undertake four round-the-World cruises for them. The first of these was to begin on the 14th June, 2003. Thus, into her forty eighth year of service, the venerable ship would be visiting many places in the World for the first time.

Initially, it was believed that *Topaz* would be chartered for just one year and that her most likely rôle after that would be as an hotel ship for the duration of the 2004 Athens Olympic Games. However, the Peace Boat organisation firmly denied these rumours, stating that their charter of the ship extended through until 2006.

On the 10th June, 2003, *Topaz* made her maiden arrival in Tokyo harbour. The short-lived TUI livery had been replaced by that of Peace Boat – written as one word in capital letters, PEACEBOAT was painted, together with their website address, at an angle across her hull. Her funnel was now dark blue and on it were the words Peace Boat in white and red flowing script. Nevertheless, the old liner seemed to rise above such indignities. (It appears that the website address was painted out before she sailed on her first Peace Boat voyage.)

Internally, she was little changed. The casino equipment was removed from what had long ago been the Tourist Class Smoking Room: now the forward end of the room was a library, whilst the greater part of it again functioned as a lounge – though on the deck plan it was referred to as 'Free Space'. The small and little-used areas either side of the disco bar were turned into a games area on the port side and a seminar room on starboard side. The largest of the shops that had been built in the former Tourist Class Lounge was transformed into the Peace Boat Centre.

On a dull and foggy morning, on the 8th August, 2003, and after an absence of over 28 years, *Topaz* sailed into New York for a 3-day stay as part of her first world cruise. She had once been a very familiar visitor to the port, but now her arrival went unremarked by other than a handful of ocean liner enthusiasts. At the end of that month, on the 31st, on a voyage that had already seen her call at a number of ports for the very first time, *Topaz* made her maiden entrance into the harbour of Vancouver. It was the first time that an 'Empress' liner had been in that port in over fifty years and her visit was blessed by glorious sunshine. The following day, *Topaz* departed on the final leg of her first-ever world cruise.

Shortly afterwards, the Peace Boat organisation announced that during a world cruise in 2004, *Topaz* would call at Piraeus on the 13th August, the first day of the Athens Olympic Games. It was also revealed that the same cruise would see the liner returning to Britain, but again this would be a first-time call – instead of either Liverpool or Southampton, her schedule had her calling at Tilbury. The last time an 'Empress' liner had been there was back in February, 1972 when the former *Empress of Canada* had departed for Miami as *Mardi Gras*. Thus it seems that the former *Empress of Britain* has brought the story of the Canadian Pacific liners full circle. It is perhaps fitting that the last operational 'Empress' should end her career in such a similar way to that in which the first 'Empress' liner, the *Empress of India*, began hers 113 years earlier.

Apart from eleven months of inactivity following the collapse of Greek Line, *Topaz* – as *Empress of Britain*, *Queen Anna Maria*, *Carnivale* and *Olympic* – has been in

In this view of *The Topaz* at Madeira, the forward extension made to her superstructure before her charter to Thomson Cruises is very evident. *Luis Miguel Correia.*

This study of *The Topaz*'s funnel shows its welded and riveted structure, the scars left by the Royal Olympic badge and the undignified logo adopted by the Thomson group after they were taken over. *Luís Miguel Correia.*

almost continuous operation for forty eight years, enjoying the most successful of careers. *Apollon*'s final years were not blessed with the same good luck as those of her near-sister. Nevertheless, for the greater part of her forty-plus years of service, she too had enjoyed considerable success. There is no doubt that both ships will be best remembered for their many years as *Mardi Gras* and *Carnivale* under the Carnival Cruise Lines banner. It was by some strange good fortune that Ted Arison was persuaded to take the journey out to the rather desolate areas of the docks at Tilbury to inspect the laid-up *Empress of Canada*. It was a journey that shaped his future, the future of the ship and, ultimately, the future of the cruise industry itself.

While the origins of both *Empress of Canada* and *Empress of Britain* as very British trans-Atlantic liners have remained obvious to the very end, it was through the vision of Ted Arison that the former 'Empresses' were transformed into two of the most popular cruise ships, establishing Carnival Cruise Lines as the most significant force in the industry. Consequently, *Empress of Canada* and *Empress of Britain* became two of the most important liners ever built. To have sailed aboard one of the last 'Empresses' was a privilege not easily forgotten.

Topaz at Tokyo after her surprise charter by the Peace Boat organisation for a series of world cruises. Her new livery is not flattering but it is splendid to know that, after nearly a half-century of service, she is still so active. *Ken Murayama.*